Praise for *Assessing with Respect*

Steeped in research but practical for any educator, *Assessing with Respect* provides clear, student-centered approaches to assessment and grading that are meaningful and edifying for students. Sackstein takes a whole child approach, focusing on so much more than what's on the test. Instead, she takes on hot topics, difficult issues, and outdated thinking by describing powerful, doable practices that accelerate learning and deepen relationships with students. A must-read for any educator!

—*Kara Vandas, author and consultant*

Starr Sackstein is a reflective practitioner who clearly practices what she so passionately preaches. In this honest and insightful book, she challenges educators to take an honest look at past and current practices used in schools and to rethink why and how we assess students. Masterfully weaving in personal experiences and practitioner vignettes, Sackstein presents innovative ideas and practical strategies to better meet students' emotional and academic needs and make real change in the ways we assess them.

—*Evan Robb, principal, author, and speaker*

Sackstein's experience, expertise, and commitment to deepening her own self-awareness will serve novice and seasoned educators alike as they begin to consider what assessment can—and should—mean for learners and learning. This book calls on us to move into this work with bravery and humility, so that we may do better—together.

—*Angela Stockman, author, teacher, and professional learning service provider*

Assessing with Respect addresses the complexities that both teachers and administrators face when it comes to assessment. Too often as educators, we do not discuss the emotional responses that students have to assessment and grading. Sackstein not only unpacks the elements necessary to meet students' social and emotional needs but also provides a framework for providing meaningful feedback that leads to improved academic results. Each chapter provides practical and realistic takeaways and thought-provoking reflection questions. Every teacher and administrator who wants to build better relationships with students and help students take ownership of their learning should have this book in their personal library.

—*Dr. Basil Marin, assistant principal, Chamblee Charter High School*

ASSESSING
with RESPECT

ASSESSING with RESPECT

Everyday Practices That Meet Students' Social and Emotional Needs

Starr Sackstein

ASCD

Alexandria, Virginia USA

1703 N. Beauregard St. • Alexandria, VA 22311-1714 USA
Phone: 800-933-2723 or 703-578-9600 • Fax: 703-575-5400
Website: www.ascd.org • E-mail: member@ascd.org
Author guidelines: www.ascd.org/write

Ranjit Sidhu, *CEO & Executive Director*; Penny Reinart, *Chief Impact Officer*; Stefani Roth, *Publisher*; Genny Ostertag, *Director, Content Acquisitions*; Julie Houtz, *Director, Book Editing & Production*; Miriam Calderone, *Editor*; Thomas Lytle, *Creative Director*; Donald Ely, *Art Director*; Georgia Park, *Senior Graphic Designer*; Cynthia Stock, *Typesetter*; Kelly Marshall, *Manager, Project Management*; Shajuan Martin, *E-Publishing Specialist*

All web links in this book are correct as of the publication date below but may have become inactive or otherwise modified since that time. If you notice a deactivated or changed link, please e-mail books@ascd.org with the words "Link Update" in the subject line. In your message, please specify the web link, the book title, and the page number on which the link appears.

PAPERBACK ISBN: 978-1-4166-2997-9   ASCD product #121023   n3/21
PDF E-BOOK ISBN: 978-1-4166-2999-3; see Books in Print for other formats.
Quantity discounts are available: e-mail programteam@ascd.org or call 800-933-2723, ext. 5773, or 703-575-5773. For desk copies, go to www.ascd.org/deskcopy.

Library of Congress Cataloging-in-Publication Data

Names: Sackstein, Starr, author.
Title: Assessing with respect : everyday practices that meet students'
   social and emotional needs / Starr Sackstein.
Description: Alexandria, VA USA : ASCD, 2021. | Includes bibliographical
   references and index.
Identifiers: LCCN 2020050103 (print) | LCCN 2020050104 (ebook) | ISBN
   9781416629979 (paperback) | ISBN 9781416629993 (pdf)
Subjects: LCSH: Social learning—Study and teaching. | Emotional
   intelligence—Study and teaching. | Teacher-student relationships. |
   Educational equalization. | Motivation in education.
Classification: LCC LC192.4 .S23 2021 (print) | LCC LC192.4 (ebook) | DDC
   370.15—dc23
LC record available at https://lccn.loc.gov/2020050103
LC ebook record available at https://lccn.loc.gov/2020050104

29 28 27 26 25 24 23 22 21   1 2 3 4 5 6 7 8 9 10 11 12

*To all my teachers who truly saw me, and not just
the work I submitted: Thank you for recognizing a shy
but precocious learner who was so much more than
just a score or a grade.*

*To all my students who have shared their humanity
and trusted my nontraditional methods: We have truly
had each other's best interests in our hearts.*

*To all my colleagues, wherever you are on your assessment
journey: It is never too late to do something differently.
Give yourselves grace when you make mistakes,
but remember to learn while you model the process.*

ASSESSING *with* RESPECT

Everyday Practices That Meet Students' Social and Emotional Needs

Foreword

I believe that, as educators, we all enter the profession with this valuable and honorable mission: to have a profound and positive impact on students, families, colleagues, and the greater learning community. This mission can sometimes feel impossible and overwhelming with so many factors and challenges pushing against us, our students, families, and communities. Systemic racism and the oppression it creates are real factors that affect the mental and physical health of individuals, families, and communities.

Our students walk into the school building as complex human beings who bring forth not only their innate gifts and talents but also the joy and toll of their life experiences. Some may arrive with the aura of love and care, some with the sense that what they receive is never enough, some with a bitter sense of the world, some with the hope for better. To fulfill our mission as educators, we are tasked with supporting students in meeting academic requirements while providing for the social, emotional, and physical ones as well. We do this while simultaneously caring for our own needs and those of our loved ones.

How do we meet the individual needs of self, family, students, staff, and our communities? How do we push beyond the skin in which we live, the seat in which we sit, and the experiences that shaped us in order to meet the needs of students and staff who are so very different from us? How do we support the social, emotional, physical, and academic growth of students, staff, and community?

Starr Sackstein, and those who contributed to this book, provide educators with the answers to these questions. Right now is the time, and learning communities are the place where we must wrap around students and families, providing the academic, emotional, physical, and social support needed.

Although there is no formal oath for educators comparable to the Hippocratic oath for doctors, we should all strive to be ethical in our personal and professional lives and commit to do no harm to those we serve. Education is an honorable profession, as we accept the responsibility for the intellectual, emotional, social, and even physical development of our nation's youth. We may not realize it when we step into our first classroom, but educators choose the responsibility to provide all students and their parents—especially the most vulnerable and marginalized—with high-quality educational programming that includes comprehensive support and services.

Our Black, Brown, and Indigenous students are the most likely to drop out of school and to enter the juvenile justice system, which deposits them into the school-to-prison pipeline. As educators and educational leaders, we must become leaders of equity. We must investigate and accept how it is that we have systematically failed our students, so that we can transform these systems. Our students need and deserve an educational experience in which they, and each member of the learning community, feel recognized, valued, and accepted—simply for being who they are.

My decision to become an educator was two-pronged. First, I was a single 21-year-old mother of two little girls, and I wanted nothing more than to provide stability for them. Second, I wanted the opportunity to be the educator that my friends and I had needed, especially during the early 1990s when I was in high school. We were all products of the circumstances and neighborhoods created by the system of racism upon which our country is built. One of my friends was abandoned by her mom and lived with her boyfriend and his family. Another sold drugs out of her locker for her boyfriend. One girl, who had been repeatedly sexually abused by different men her mother brought into the house, would leave school to hook up with men at a nearby park. One of my best friends confided in me that her mother's boyfriend, who was married and paid their rent, had been abusing her, and she was worried that her little sister was next. It was easier to get high or drunk in school than it was any-where else due to availability and lack of concern from our teachers and the school staff. The adults within the school walls didn't seem to know how to connect with us, so we continued on our paths with no meaning-ful interventions. We were able to maneuver our way through classes and accountability by doing the bare minimum and lying when necessary, and every time our lies were accepted by school counselors and teachers. Maybe it wasn't acceptance, but resignation. Even if we had told the truth of our realities, the system was not set up to respond. So when I was 21 and preparing to move from community college to San Diego State Uni-versity, I had to finally choose a major. It was with my daughters and my high school experience in mind that I chose to become an educator and commit to the honorable mission of making a difference.

My professional life has provided so much for me in the way of personal and professional growth. The experiences in the K–12 learning system taught me a few key things that I have been able to carry with me into all aspects of my life (including work). These learnings include the following:

- It is imperative to continue doing the work of reflecting on my experience, my actions, and my motivations.
    - I attribute this work to how well I know myself and my ability to authentically enter any space.
    - I have committed to never leaving a conversation or a space without saying or doing what my heart and spirit call me to say or do.
    - By diving into my own journey, which can be horrendously painful, I ultimately get to know myself better, which helps me connect with others.
- Every person, regardless of age, joins me on this journey as a whole human being with a lifetime of experiences that should be honored. In my role I have chosen to do the following:
    - Listen to them and communicate how valuable they are.
    - Provide the guidance needed, when invited to, to promote their intellectual and personal growth.

- As much as I hope to affect others, I am the one who has been truly changed by being allowed to join others on the journey.
  - Every time someone shares a piece of themselves with me, they are honoring me with a gift of themselves. Their gift could be the sharing of pain or joy.

These foundational learnings guide my approach to life and our collective work in education. First, we must do the work within. Then we can use the knowledge of self to connect with others to begin the heavy lift of supporting individuals and learning communities. Fortunately, in this book, Starr has provided a resource to support educators in doing their work while building truly comprehensive systems of support that have the potential to transform realities for our students, families, and communities.

Marisol Rerucha

Acknowledgments

In my first teaching position, I learned a lot about myself and how much I had to learn as a teacher and as a human. Although the school was just five miles from where I grew up, the socioeconomic divide and the racial disparity were greater than I had realized. Each day, I learned something new about my students and myself. I made terrible assumptions that would later smack reality across my face, and I came to see that I faced a chasm that would require a considerable amount of learning if I wanted to become a better person and educator.

Over the years, I have had many teachers and friends who have helped me explore my implicit bias, privilege, and ignorance. Although I have been working for a long time on improving my understanding, I can never truly know what it means to be a person of color. What I can do is continue to be an anti-racist and an ally for those who don't have my luxury of privilege.

I truly appreciate those who have helped me look in the mirror and recognize uncomfortable things about myself, who have had difficult conversations with me when they didn't have to, and who have pointed me in the right direction in terms of what to read, whom to listen to, and how to dialogue when the time came. I know I still have a lot to learn, and I'm open and ready to engage in those conversations.

This book only scratches the surface of the topic of the relationship between assessment and social and emotional learning, but I hope it will introduce the idea to those of you who are new to this work and provide enough resources for additional consideration. Although it didn't start out as a book about equity, the current climate dictated that it not ignore some evident realities. For those who helped me realize my own gaps of knowledge and begin to fill them, I am grateful.

Thank you to the countless people of color who have taught me over the years about grace and anger and humility. I appreciate those of you who have taken the time to talk to me frankly and help me realize I shouldn't punish myself too much for not knowing more, as this is a life's journey and not something I can accomplish in one sitting. Those who have helped me include students who taught me about their lives and freely invited me in. Others include the scholars whose work I have read and will continue to read as I move forward on this journey.

A big thank-you to Marisol Rerucha for sharing your story and being a part of my learning. Thank you to Angela Stockman for the care, kindness, and support you provided as I struggled through writing this book. It has been a tremendous learning experience, and your knowledge and thoughtful feedback helped make it something I'm really proud of.

Thank you to my Core Collaborative family—Dr. Paul Bloomberg and Tony Francouer, Alison Cox and Donnie Luehring, Isaiah McGee and Isaac Wells, Sarah Stevens and Lori Cook—for your willingness to contribute to the book in whatever way you could. I put up the bat signal, and you all answered in your own way. I appreciate you all.

Thanks to the other contributors: Dr. John Castronova, Jessica Cimini-Samuels, Zak Cohen, Mark Erlenwein, Greg Fredericks, Allison Hamilton, Katrina Letter, Natalie McCutchen, Chrissy Romano, and Faith Tripp.

A big thank-you to former students who also answered my call when I put it out there, and to 8th grade teacher Andi Jackson, who saw one of my Facebook posts and got her students involved, too.

Much of the assessment work I have done is in service of students like my son, Logan Miller, who generously shared some of his experiences with me for this book. I'm super-proud of you, Logan, and no grade will ever define you or your capacity to succeed.

Last but certainly not least is a big thank-you to my husband, Charlie Anstadt, whose patience and contribution to my life exceed the word limit for this book. You are both a calming and an exciting influence, and I'm so lucky to be on this journey with you.

Introduction

Not everything that is faced can be changed,
but nothing can be changed until it is faced.

—James Baldwin

When I signed on to write this book, times were different. Although I
believed strongly that assessment and the social and emotional needs of
our students needed to be tied together, I couldn't possibly have pre-
dicted the way the world would turn in the months that followed.

Living in social-distancing isolation because of the COVID-19
pandemic has been an eye-opening experience. Emotionally, I've been
all over the place, sometimes inside of an hour, feeling anxiety about the
unknown, fear about loved ones, concern for my son and coworkers—
not to mention the sometimes debilitating lack of motivation because of
circumstances beyond my control.

And yet I'm among the privileged—and always have been, despite
what may have felt like momentous impediments that life has thrown
my way and the silent, not-so-obvious home situations that my teachers probably didn't know about, as I worked so hard to conceal them.
School was my sanctuary from the challenges I experienced at home, and
despite the zip code I grew up in and the support of a two-parent house-
hold, challenges did exist.

Now I have access to the internet, several electronic devices, a car,
a home, enough food, and not least of all, my health and a supportive,
available family. My job is essential and can be done safely from home.

Perhaps I haven't been eating or sleeping as well as I could be, and that has an impact on my ability to work effectively. In fact, this situation has made it hard for me to write. Writing, one of those things that has always been a stabilizer and has come easily to me, has become something I will never take for granted again. And, in the way we don't appreciate those things that do come easily, I've often wondered during this experience if this is how my students felt when they were asked to write but simply couldn't.

Our students, colleagues, and their families may not have the benefits that are more common among the privileged, and therefore, how we relate to one another has to be from a place of empathy and care, not judgment. Beyond empathy, however, there needs to be a profound acknowledgment that, although we try to truly understand the experiences of others, the depth of the challenges that many individuals, including people of color, have faced is beyond intellectual comprehension. We must continue to question, remain curious, and try to be better supporters and allies of our fellow human beings.

As an educator, a mom, and a human being, I've watched school systems struggle to meet the needs of all learners while often not having the resources, including training, to do an adequate job on any level. This is not the fault of families or individual educators, but a systemic cancer that has been plaguing schools in the United States for a long time; the COVID-19 pandemic simply illuminated the elephant in the room that not enough people had acknowledged.

Although we are all invested in helping students learn, we haven't always done a good job of considering all of the aspects of how and why that happens. What are the optimal conditions for learning to occur in an authentic and meaningful way for all students? How do we ensure, as educators at every level, as well as systemically, that we are doing everything we can to equitably attend to the needs of *all* children, as they deserve to be nurtured? Have we considered our own privilege and how that colors our ability to help those who need our help most? Whose voices are we listening to, and why?

The means by which we assess our students says a great deal about what we value and also shines a light on who stands to gain the most from those values. As educators, we must be cognizant of who is making decisions and what the implications of those decisions are for the way we assess and then label our students, in turn creating a path of potential paralysis. In other words, when we label our students, we pigeonhole them, sometimes making it impossible for them to transcend the labels. They hear what we tell them, internalize it, and then believe that this who they are, for better or for worse.

This book is intended to help leaders and other educators consider their assessment practices within a context of teaching social and emotional skills so that students develop positive learning dispositions and systems honor the dignity of the learning of all students. Our goal should not be to test and grade children to put them in a hierarchy for potential future roles of dominance or subordination—or even for the sake of sheer efficiency. It is our responsibility as educators to see children in a holistic sense and find ways that best allow them to be successful.

I have learned through researching this book that some people are critically examining social and emotional learning (SEL), and that critique has merit. Keeping in mind the Common Core, trying to develop standards around social and emotional skills becomes problematic when we all have different definitions for things like "self-management" and "regulation." The National Equity Project has resources that are helpful in working through this language and coming to understanding (see www.nationalequityproject.org). And as educators, we also have to be cognizant of critically questioning the things we read and do and consider what the impact is on the marginalized folks we work with, trying as hard as possible to not cause further harm.

My background in alternative assessment and assessment reform coupled with my research on social and emotional learning has made it clear to me that we have to take a deeper look into this important overlap. During my research, I came across the following five core SEL competencies developed by the Collaborative for Academic, Social, and Emotional Learning (CASEL, 2020):

- **Self-awareness** concerns our ability to recognize our feelings, name them, and then identify the impact they have on our ability to learn, connect, react, and so on. In terms of assessment, self-awareness comes in the form of reflection and students' ability to articulate what they know and can do using evidence from their learning. Helping students understand where they are in their learning helps them better inform us about what they need.

- **Self-management** involves the regulation of our feelings and our ability to organize and motivate. This is where we think about goal setting and accountability. Building on reflection, students are able to take feedback from formative learning experiences and apply it to their own goal setting. This is how we teach students to track their learning, set goals, and develop an understanding of self-assessment.

- **Social awareness** is about perspective and our ability to empathize. Additionally, it is about cultural awareness and diversity, and in the case of education, matters of equity. In the assessment realm, social awareness is about feedback and assessment from peers. As we teach students to work with one another and build better learning environments, we create an intentional space where challenging conversations can be had and we can all grow as learners. The way we respond to people and provide feedback should align with what we understand of them as whole individuals.

- **Relationship skills** involve building sustainable and healthy relationships that connect us to one another. Collaboration and communication are key to this competency. In our classrooms and in assessment conversations in particular, this competency is all about how we facilitate students working together, giving them the tools to problem-solve and listen to one another's voices with empathy and commitment to understanding. By creating an atmosphere in which students have multiple opportunities to dive deeply into these relationship skills, we prepare them for a life of easier communication with the people they will work with in the future.

- **Responsible decision making** is all about making good choices by being able to take stock of situations and consider possible outcomes. It is about identifying issues, problem solving, reflecting, and taking action. For assessment, this competency involves helping students identify what must be done and providing opportunities to help them make better choices. Rather than stepping in when students don't agree, we can allow them to work through disagreements and then reflect on how those conversations helped to improve or hinder their learning. Additionally, this competency will be a part of project-based learning, as students will need to not only manage their time, but also help their teams be successful.

SEL has come under scrutiny from people of color, as several of the practices can continue to marginalize students. Because of this concern, people have begun to explore CASEL's framework through a lens of equity. A November 2018 Frameworks Brief from the Assessment Work Group (managed and staffed by CASEL) states:

> Consistent with the pursuit of educational equity, we recently offered the concept of *transformational SEL* to reflect our interest in making explicit issues such as power, privilege, prejudice, discrimination, social justice, empowerment, and self-determination in the field of SEL. Transformative SEL connotes a process whereby students and teachers build strong, respectful relationships founded on an appreciation of similarities and differences, learn to critically examine root causes of inequity, and develop collaborative solutions to community and societal problems. (Jagers, Rivas-Drake, & Borowski, 2018, p. 3) (emphasis in original)

CASEL's core competencies for social and emotional learning align with Costa and Kallick's (2014) dispositions for learning, which define a number of mental habits that help us with competencies and life in general. All these things can and should be taught and need to be an integral part of how we work with students of all ages to ensure a culture of belonging, as suggested by Cobb and Krownapple's (2019) "dignity framework" in their book *Belonging Through a Culture of Dignity*. Once we determine the needs of our students, build a culture of belonging, and honor the dignity of those we teach as well as those of us doing the teaching, we can begin to build better learning environments where students can flourish and assessment can be more comprehensive.

In this book, Chapters 1 through 4 address the CASEL competencies and their overlap with what schools need to be doing to better assess learning while promoting the social and emotional well-being of students. The chapters also provide classroom strategies for building these whole-child learning and assessing experiences, keeping in mind that assessment consists not only of end-of-unit exams or summative writing assignments, but also everyday formative experiences. Chapters 5 and 6 address the topics of grades and personalized assessment, respectively.

It's important to remember that *assessment is* not a static thing, but an action—an ongoing formative process that we engage in continually to ensure all students are getting what they need. It is an educator's responsibility to assess students for learning on a daily basis. Doing so is as important for teachers as it is for students. Students need to be able to discuss what they know and can do and how they know it, and we need to be able to see how well our instruction is working and what we need to adjust so that all students can learn effectively. Grades, like tests, are only one part of the story—a small part that ends up getting magnified for ease of discussion. These summative experiences often shed little light on what kids know and can do—and worse, they seldom contribute to future learning.

Feedback, reflection, and personalized approaches to learning that take into account the needs of each student are what truly develop effective learners. These strategies provide ongoing opportunities for students to apply new knowledge and feedback, to practice, to set goals, and to develop skill sets and content knowledge with the help of teachers and peers. This approach is what we need to be focusing on.

1

Building Relationships to Support Learning

Learning can be a scary proposition for some students, and when their basic needs aren't met, the likelihood of doing it well is markedly low. To help all students succeed, teachers and school communities need to build deeper connections with students, enabling better understanding of not only surface needs but also core social and emotional needs that can affect learning in many ways. Although it may sound like a cliché to say that relationships are key to learning, the idea has become a cliché because it is true. We simply can't undervalue the importance of intentionally building relationships in schools to increase student success.

Aside from the inherent benefits of relational trust, schools that build great relationships develop assessment-capable learners who not only succeed in the conventional sense—completing classwork, contributing productively to class discussions, developing knowledge and skills at or above standards—but also potentially actualize the best versions of themselves. Classrooms that make relationships a high priority create the conditions for deeper curiosity and greater accessibility to individual student and teacher expertise. Quality relationships can increase a student's ability to learn more deeply by allowing for positive risk taking. How much students will risk in their own learning can shape the way we construct and conduct assessments throughout the year.

Relationship building requires that we explore ourselves, including our personal biases and how they affect our ability to work with students. Taking a deeper look at what we know and value and how we express our beliefs will affect our ability both to build better relationships with all invested parties—relationships that are more empathetic and humble—and to model that process.

This chapter addresses CASEL's core competencies of relationship skills and social awareness. CASEL (2020) defines *relationship skills* as follows:

> The abilities to establish and maintain healthy and supportive relationships and to effectively navigate settings with diverse individuals and groups. This includes the capacities to communicate clearly, listen actively, cooperate, work collaboratively to problem solve and negotiate conflict constructively, navigate settings with differing social and cultural demands and opportunities, provide leadership, and seek or offer help when needed.

It defines *social awareness* as follows:

> The abilities to understand the perspectives of and empathize with others, including those from diverse backgrounds, cultures, and contexts. This includes the capacities to feel compassion for others, understand broader historical and social norms for behavior in different settings, and recognize family, school, and community resources and supports.

Addressing the two competencies together acknowledges their interlocking and complementary characteristics. Social awareness is a foundational component of relationship skills, and, in turn, building relationships contributes to continual development of social awareness.

Teacher-Student Relationships

Often, even before the first day of school, teacher-student relationships are developing through word-of-mouth by students who came before. Teachers who are challenging to get along with are identified as such by reputation. Although I am not suggesting that we seek friendships with our students or that we shouldn't be firm in our expectations and demeanor, I am suggesting that what students experience in our behavior matters, especially if they are ever going to see us as allies and advocates for them. Of course, in our efforts to become better allies and advocates, we must recognize the thin line between the intention to help and the harmful idea of the "white man's burden"—the notion, derived from 19th century colonization, that it is white people's responsibility to "uplift" people of color.

Kids immediately size up the demeanor we project (and what we hope to accomplish by that demeanor). Teachers who seek to be seen as a "dictator" can expect students to fear them and, as a result, to not fully trust them. That isn't to say students won't appreciate the teacher's expertise or admit to learning from the teacher later, but rather that we need to strike a balance to develop good professional relationships with students, showing care *and* creating structure.

When we model how we would like students to be—honest, straightforward, engaged, and humane—students respond in kind. Taking time at the beginning of the school year to develop relationships with each student, beyond just knowing names, will increase the opportunities for personalized learning and ultimately increase learning over time.

Strategies for Developing Appropriate, Trusting Relationships

Regardless of what students hear about teachers, first impressions matter. If possible, draft a letter before school begins, inviting students to a shared learning space. Welcome them, and be clear about expectations. Use language that supports the message you're conveying, and clearly communicate your excitement for teaching them. If you like, add information about the kinds of learning that will occur in class. For older students, attaching a syllabus to your welcome letter can help them see the scope of learning and ties to assessment throughout the year. (See the appendix for examples of a syllabus I have used.) Figure 1.1 is an example of a letter I wrote for high school students and parents/caregivers.

Beyond being the first official greeting, a welcome letter sets the tone for the year to come. If you're working with younger students, don't be afraid to be playful and friendly. See Figure 1.2 for an example from Natalie McCutchen, a 7th grade math teacher at Franklin-Simpson Middle School in Franklin, Kentucky. Note that Natalie ends her letter with questions that will help her better plan how to create relevant examples,

FIGURE 1.1

Welcome Letter for High School

Hello, Students and Parents/Caregivers:

Welcome to your senior year. Students, this is your opportunity to really prepare for the next phase of your lives, seriously thinking about the kind of students you want to be and become in the future. It no longer matters who you were in the past or what mistakes you may have made; this year is about establishing who you will be.

The AP Literature class you will be taking is a rigorous one that promises to both challenge and prepare you for that next phase of your lives. Traditionally, some students might think that senior year is supposed to be easy after the work put forth since freshman year, but I don't believe that to be true. I'm not saying not to have a good time with your newfound "almost freedom," but I am saying I wouldn't be doing you a favor to let you slack off. I want you to feel prepared for what comes next once you are on your own.

That said, I'm so excited to have you all in my classroom. You will be given a syllabus with due dates for all assignments. We will go over it on the first day of class, and you will be expected to adhere to this schedule. You will have minimal reminders. Adhering to schedules with minimal reminders is what you can expect next year, when you are in college. As adults, you must be responsible for your choices and your work. At the beginning of the year, I will likely reach out to your parents/caregivers after I talk with you first to ensure that communication is clear and they are in the loop about the expectations outlined in this letter. I want to treat you like college students, and therefore you will need to take the initiative and reach out to me when you need help. I am here to help you and want to do so, but tracking you down is not how it works when you get to college.

I'm looking forward to creating an engaging learning environment with each of you, one that is filled with your varied personalities and perspectives.

Welcome to your senior year!

All smiles,
Ms. Sackstein, NBCT

Parents/caregivers, please e-mail me when you receive this letter so that I have your up-to-date e-mail addresses. E-mail is the easiest way for me to reach you.

Our class website will have all the resources students need. I will post supplemental information and updates periodically. The syllabus is already posted there, and a calendar of due dates will be posted soon. If you ever have any questions, please don't hesitate to reach out to me. Looking forward to a great year!

FIGURE 1.2

Welcome Letter for Middle School

Dear _____,

Hello! My name is Mrs. McCutchen, and I will have the privilege of being your teacher for the upcoming school year.

I graduated from Western Kentucky University in May 2005 with a Bachelor of Science degree in middle grades education; in May 2011, I graduated with my master's degree in administration.

 I have a wonderful husband named Mac, and we have been married for 11 years. We have three amazing children: Natalya, who is 9 years old; Macaiah, who is 7 years old; and Nathan, who is 3 years old.

I am excited about the upcoming school year and look forward to meeting you. I have many fun and exciting things planned for this school year, and I hope that you will find my class and math enjoyable.

My main goal is for you to achieve greatness. I want you to succeed with learning math and in whatever you try to do.

 I will teach you not only math, but also important values such as respect, responsibility, and confidence.

I believe that all my students are great people and are capable of learning. All I ask of you is to do your best, and I will be happy.

I look forward to getting to know you better as the year progresses. Let's have a great year.

If you ever need help with anything, please call or e-mail me.

Sign up to receive texts about class info!

P.S. Don't forget Open House is Monday, August 12, at 6:00. Hope to see you there!!

P.P.S. Here is your first assignment! You are going to write a one-page letter about yourself by answering the following questions:

- What did you learn or learn to do this summer?
- What things do you do that help your family survive or succeed?
- What skills do you have that no one else in your family has?
- What is each person in your family good at?
- How do you make friends?
- What do you want to know more about?
- Where and whom do you learn from?
- Tell me what's on your bookshelf, e-reader, tablet, Facebook, Instagram, or Snapchat right now, and what it tells me about you as a person.
- What do you do when you're faced with a really interesting or tough-to-solve problem?
- What do you want the world to know and think about you, both now and in the future?

Source: Courtesy Natalie McCutchen, Franklin-Simpson Middle School, Franklin, KY. Used with permission.

engage students with personal connections to their interests, and create better assessments based on what she learns.

Figure 1.3 shows an example from an elementary school teacher, Chrissy Romano, who teaches 2nd grade at Nellie K. Parker Elementary School in Hackensack, New Jersey. Notice how Chrissy's letter conveys a friendly tone by encouraging her students to enjoy a variety of summer activities and be ready to share their experiences when they come to her class.

Although welcome letters can set the tone before school begins, the first day of school is important as well. The goal is for students to leave your classroom feeling excited about returning the next day and coming home with rave reviews for their parents or caregivers. Here are some tips for the first day of school:

- Make sure the room is clean and inviting before students arrive so that they can see the care you put into your shared space.
- Welcome students at the door with a smile.
- Focus on getting to know each other, *not* reviewing school and classroom rules and procedures, which sends the wrong message and takes up valuable class time. You can address these matters later in the first week and also develop classroom norms *with* your students, which is likely to result in more student buy-in.
- Use icebreakers that can help you get to know your students and them to know one another. Choose activities that get students out of their seats and moving around, like the one shown in Figure 1.4.
- Do a gallery walk around the learning space and ask students what they notice as, together, you imagine what an ideal learning space looks like. This activity can lead to students "designing" the classroom in a way that addresses different learning preferences.

Of course, the first week of school isn't the only opportunity you will have to make an impression and build relationships; it's just the start. Remember to stay consistent but flexible as you get to know your kids better. Pay attention to body language and who students spend time with. Become aware of which students are more assertive than others,

FIGURE 1.3

Welcome Letter for Elementary School

Nellie K. Parker Elementary School

Ms. Romano

2nd Grade—Room 307

Welcome to 2nd grade!

I hope you and your family are enjoying your time away from school. With the time you have left of the summer, here are some things I would love for you to do if you can.

- Spend time with FAMILY and FRIENDS.
- CREATE or BUILD something.
- Be CURIOUS and WONDER about all the things you encounter.
- READ for fun.
- PLAY! Play outside, play inside, play board games, play cards— just play!
- Use your IMAGINATION every day.
- Have FUN! Fun is what summer break is all about.

You may want to take pictures of cool things you do over the summer, or write or draw about them. Use any way to capture your adventures so you can remember them to share when we get back to school.

Relax, enjoy, and get ready for an awesome year in 2nd grade!

Can't wait to meet you!

—Ms. Romano

Source: Courtesy Chrissy Romano, Nellie K. Parker Elementary School, Hackensack, NJ. Used with permission.

FIGURE 1.4

Icebreaker Activity: "Find Someone Who . . ."

This icebreaker can be done in a number of ways. Students can interview their classmates to find out which items apply to them and have them sign or initial the item, or the items can be presented as a Bingo grid. Depending on the age of the students, you can adjust the specifics to things that they would likely have done.

Find someone who . . .

1. Traveled this summer
2. Loves to read
3. Knows what they want to be when they grow up
4. "Lives" on social media
5. Watches sports on TV
6. Plays a sport
7. Plays a musical instrument
8. Loves to eat
9. Is into fitness
10. Loves baseball
11. Travels by public transportation to school
12. Is a morning person
13. Loves coffee
14. Is an only child
15. Has a pet
16. Saw at least two movies this summer
17. Watches reality television
18. Plays Candy Crush or Trivia Crack
19. Has attended a sporting event
20. Has been to another country
21. Has a job
22. Loves the beach
23. Knows what college they would like to attend
24. Likes vegetables
25. Has a best friend in this class
26. Knows how to ride a bike
27. Writes a blog/considers themselves a writer
28. Wants to change the world
29. Is interested in politics
30. Has read a classic novel
31. Loves technology
32. Knows how to use phones for learning
33. Can work with their hands
34. Lives with extended family
35. Can speak another language

and find classroom roles that will allow them to feel like leaders without dominating to the point of excluding other voices. Notice which students are inherently quiet, and engage in conversations to understand why this is so. Don't allow students who are somewhere in between to sit patiently while others carry the weight. Talk with individual students on their way in and out of class, asking about their day or weekend and expressing genuine interest in their answers.

During the first month of school, conduct a learning assessment that allows students to share how they learn best. Various websites include surveys that students can take to help them articulate how they like to learn, such as EducationPlanner.org. Surveys such as these can be a starting point for students who may have trouble articulating their learning preferences.

Regardless of the content you teach, ask students to write a short piece or draw a picture about themselves or an experience they have had that they think will help you better understand them as a person and a learner. Note what they share, and ask clarifying questions. As a model, share something you've written yourself that tells them what you want them to know about you as a person and a teacher. You don't need to share too much personal information, but the more open you are, the more students will open up to you.

How Deeper Relationships Help Learning Thrive

Taking the time to develop deeper relationships with students will nurture the learning environment. Your students will trust you and therefore will be more willing to take risks when you ask them to step out of their comfort zones. The knowledge you gain about your students can inform your lesson design, formative learning experiences, and eventually summative assessments. Continuing to foster deep connections is likely to encourage students to not only seek your help when they need it but also follow your suggestions when you provide them.

Ultimately, the time you invest in building these important relationships will pay dividends in student commitment to learning and buy-in in the future, especially if the cultural backgrounds of your students differ from yours. Taking the time to understand the backstories of individual students—where they come from, who they are in every sense, what their socioeconomic situation is—will help you make better decisions and engender continuing trust.

Additionally, the importance of expressing vulnerability—for example, admitting when you don't know something or asking for help—can't be overestimated. Allowing yourself to be vulnerable with students as learners and human beings opens the door to modeling how this vulnerability draws people closer together. It is an opportunity to demonstrate the trust it takes to share personal information and to give students a sense of the value you place on your relationship with them.

Student-Student Relationships

Teacher-student relationships aren't the only ones that matter. The connection and collaboration of students with their peers is also essential. The way we allow students to learn speaks to our values, and building a culture in which students treat one another with respect, dignity, and empathy will further build the trust needed to help learning thrive.

If we want students to trust one another—which we do, because trust is an essential element of collaboration and group work, peer review and feedback, and classroom discussion—we need to make sure they know how to behave and interact with one another. In her book *Culturally Responsive Teaching and the Brain,* Zaretta Hammond (2015) discusses how we can create collaborative environments with equitable learning time by using protocols that ensure that all voices are heard and none are prized more than others. It's not enough to tell students to respect one another; we must take a deeper look at how we form collaborations and then make sure that everyone in these groups participates in the learning.

You can facilitate this kind of equity by co-constructing with students the success criteria for what respect looks like in a classroom. Ask students to reflect on their ability to adhere to the criteria and why doing so matters. Provide feedback that helps them grow in their ability to demonstrate respect.

As you and your students are getting to know each other at the beginning of the school year, allow students to form their own partnerships. Note whom students gravitate toward and what the learning looks like when partners are together. Are these successful partnerships? How do you know? If they aren't, how could you improve the partnerships?

Students deserve to be involved in classroom decision making (recall that responsible decision making is another SEL competency), and so they should be clear on their options and how their choices will affect future learning. Additionally, they are going to be playing a big supporting role in the learning and the assessing of themselves and their peers, so they need to trust one another as much as they trust you, if not more.

Strategies for Building Constructive Relationships

Obviously, we want students to be friends, but friendship is not what I'm talking about here. Learning to be a vital part of a team or group is an important aspect of other kinds of learning, so it is important to promote a culture that encourages students to develop effective collaboration skills. Not every student likes to work in a group, and although we want to honor students' preferences, collaboration is an important life skill that is not inherent and must be taught.

In my book *Peer Feedback in the Classroom* (Sackstein, 2017), I speak about developing expert groups that allow students to effectively promote one another's learning. The concept involves teaching small groups to be experts in a particular skill or task. The groups then become the go-to students for that skill or task throughout the year, simultaneously continuing to increase their expertise through their own work. It takes at least two months to really know students' strengths and challenges, and at that point you can carefully select groups with up to five members. Because the groups may be working together on a variety of activities for the rest of the year, ensuring the right balance and dynamic is essential. That isn't to say adjustments can't be made, but changing group composition shouldn't be the default approach.

When preparing students to be experts, you first need to help them address their individual challenges related to their assigned area, which means also helping them to deal with their vulnerability with peers. As they reflect on their strengths and challenges, have them share with the group so they can develop a collective understanding of how best to work together. Sharing will also help them know what to aim for in their own work and what to expect from others. In addition, as I note in *Peer Feedback,*

> Make sure to provide students with reading and research in the specific area they are working on that is appropriate for their level of mastery. Differentiate the materials as needed. For example, consider a couple of resources that say the same thing but in different ways. For my own writing workshops, in addition to sending students a brief explanation of each expert group's role, I taught mini-lessons to the whole class on these specific areas. I also provided resources from the Purdue OWL (Online Writing Lab) and encouraged students to ask specific questions. In addition, while we were setting up the groups, I visited with each small group, gave students time to review their small section of the paper, and answered questions as they arose. Once they are done shoring up their own expertise, students can work together to examine bodies of work found online or in a resource library in the classroom and make a bank of common mistakes or challenges to look for in their expert areas. (Sackstein, 2017, p. 83)

Creating Safe Spaces

In general, your goal should be to create safe spaces that allow and encourage students to discuss challenges with one another in productive ways and to work things out together instead of always seeking your help first. Working with people of different backgrounds is part of life, and teaching students to take responsibility—to take an interest in and advocate for one another—contributes to productive learning and life experiences.

Student-Culture Relationships

In addition to relationships with one another, students have relation-ships with the culture that their school cultivates as well as the cultures they come from. To help students understand how their personal cultures enhance the learning environment, have them share information about their backgrounds and then continually nurture an environment that honors the dignity of every member of the classroom—the students and yourself. Developing this cultural depth of knowledge should extend to how you design learning experiences and assessments, including modifying expectations as necessary to account for the needs of all learners.

Taking the time to understand others' values and beliefs contributes to our awareness of and relationship to diversity and helps to build social capital in the classroom. Students will encounter all kinds of people in their lives, and developing curiosity and deepened awareness of other cultures will enhance those relationships and diminish the likelihood of inaccurate assumptions, fears, and prejudices. It is essential to allow students to reflect on their own identities, question their own biases, and work through possible implicit biases that can create unintentional harm. Students of different perspectives, backgrounds, and cultures have something important to share that can't and shouldn't be ignored. Of course, in our efforts to include students, we must be careful to not tokenize those of different backgrounds—that is, use one student as a means for understanding all individuals who have a given background or who identify a certain way (e.g., people of color or members of the LGBTQ community)—which is both inaccurate and dangerous. When we tokenize, we are seeking inclusion but miss the mark because we are more concerned with appearances than actual inclusion.

Allowing time in class to have difficult conversations that address privilege and systemic racism can foster a sense of students and teachers as allies in an effort to ensure that each child feels heard, understood, and welcomed. Of course, I am just scratching the surface here and in no way want to suggest that a few conversations are going to correct such a big problem. Given the complexity of the challenges and prejudices that exist historically, we all must work every day to do better. This is one small way to start.

Teacher-Family Relationships

Another essential relationship that will either enhance or hurt your ability to help students is the one you cultivate with their families. As noted
earlier, we all bring more than just ourselves into our learning spaces.
Having the most complete picture possible of the learners in front of you
is essential—not to mention the fact that you will need to enlist the help
of these caregivers as partners in your students' learning.

Understanding how students behave and interact with family
members can be extremely helpful in getting some students out of their
shells. You'll note that in my high school welcome letter (Figure 1.1), I
addressed parents and caregivers as well as students. Because everyone is
on the same team, everyone needs to be on the same page about expectations, goals, and contributions to learning.

Create multiple opportunities, beyond those on the school calendar,
for family members to speak with you. Remind them that you are always
open to their questions, concerns, and involvement, and then take into
account what you learn from their insights. Find out families' preferred
method of communication—and then make sure to communicate.

Making positive phone calls once a week can be as uplifting for you
as it is for your students and their families. The effort promotes caring
bonds that can only strengthen future partnerships. Calling only when
there is a problem sets up a negative dynamic that doesn't necessarily promote families' willingness to help; it can even make a situation
adversarial. Families need to know that you have their kids' best interest
at heart, and recognizing and reaching out to share positive experiences
helps to do just that.

The extreme circumstance of the COVID-19 pandemic has made positive and communicative relationships with families more important than
ever. Being true partners in educating children requires good relationships.
You can bring families into the learning space by creating YouTube chan-
nels that share learning experiences in addition to the websites or online
classrooms facilitated by your district. Families should be privy to what
goes on during the school day at any time, not just during a crisis.

Additionally, schools can enlist cultural liaisons, whose important role is explained by Sarah W. Nelson and Patricia L. Guerra (2011) in their newsletter about cultural proficiency:

> Educators in schools serving large populations of culturally diverse students often have backgrounds that differ from the students and families they serve. This cultural mismatch can make developing strong school-community relationships a challenge. One strategy for addressing this concern is the use of a cultural liaison. A cultural liaison is someone who has standing within a community culture group and is willing to serve as a link between the community and the school. A cultural liaison helps school personnel better understand the values and norms of the community and helps community members negotiate the structures of the school system. (p. 57)

Teacher-Leadership Relationships

A big part of school culture plays out in hallways, administrative offices, and meeting spaces. Your relationships with peers and school and district leaders can model for students what to do or what not to do in some situations. Furthermore, because schools or districts often dictate which assessments must be given and how, as well as what data are to be collected, having positive relationships with key decision makers is essential to making sure that you are supported in the choices you make to best serve your students.

Ultimately, the better your relationships with building and district leaders, the more inclined you will be to speak out about the needs of your learners and advocate on their behalf. When relationships at this level break down, students and families may get misleading or conflicting messages that can only complicate the learning process. Presenting a strong, cohesive front for students and the community allows systems and the people within them to focus their time on learning rather than on dispelling misconceptions.

Leadership can promote positive relationships by having open-door policies and inviting teacher feedback related to school or districtwide initiatives. Just as in classroom communities, voices need to be honored and respected in the wider school community. Rather than having a culture in which directives are created at the top and then passed down without input, districts need to invite the voices of those who do the daily work and listen to their feedback. These open dialogues will make for more open and trusting relationships that will also help teachers improve through their observations and other initiatives. When teachers trust their leaders and leaders trust their teachers, kids win.

If leadership also provides opportunities for teachers to work together and strengthen their ties, the results can include clearer understandings of the characteristics of grade-level and content-area mastery. Teachers need time to work together, build their own collegial relationships, and come to consensus about what successful learning looks like so that all students are getting the same message.

Developing a Sense of Belonging and Honoring Differences

Although the concept has been touched upon throughout this chapter, it is important to directly acknowledge and discuss the idea of "belonging." Equitable learning spaces ensure that all participants have what they need to be successful, honoring not only academic needs but also social and emotional ones.

In their book *Belonging Through a Culture of Dignity*, Floyd Cobb and John Krownapple (2019) define belonging as

> the extent to which people feel appreciated, validated, accepted, and
> treated fairly within an environment (e.g., school, classroom, or work).
> When students feel that they belong, they aren't worried and distracted
> about being treated as a stereotype or a thin slice of their multidi-
> mensional identities (Willms, 2000). Instead, they are confident that
> they are seen as a human being, a person of value. Belonging isn't just
> a nice sentiment or a word on a Hallmark greeting card. It's a need
> that's hardwired into human beings. Like neglecting the need for food
> or water, neglecting belonging is hazardous to our health. In fact, it's
> lethal. (p. 43)

We should never ask students or teachers to omit a part of who they are so that they can be successful in our spaces. Instead, we need to find a way to embrace each person's identity and then use it for the benefit of the person and the shared space. This approach is especially applicable to the learning opportunities we provide for students. It is easy to create an assignment that may hit on particular content but doesn't allow for students to show everything they know on the topic; such an assignment could promote anxiety and frustration. Being aware of the needs of our learners helps us to develop assignments and assessment opportunities—whether they are projects or exams—that provide opportunities for voice and choice and support student success.

In my early career, before I had the teaching chops I needed to develop, I was fortunate to meet students who helped me become a better person. In my second year, I met a young woman whose background was quite different from mine. She was 17 years old, preparing for an arranged marriage, as was customary in her culture, and trying to come to terms with her sexuality. Of course, I didn't know most of that at the time. I just knew that she took refuge in my classroom, and when I needed a senior to volunteer to take control of the yearbook production, she responded.

We often had frank conversations about her family and her fears, and she often humored my incessant curiosity and tried to help me be less ignorant. I was quite young then, maybe 24, so we were almost the same age but living different lives. (We could have been friends at the time, and in fact, after she graduated we stayed in touch, and I would call her a friend now.) A closeness developed between us as she shared her art and her stories while we worked on the layout of the yearbook, and when she came out to me, I could only be supportive, knowing that her family wouldn't be.

Later she told me that few people had ever really listened to her and made her feel heard at that point in her life. My willingness to accept her as she was, without judgment, made it possible for her to speak her truth. I am grateful that I could be that person for her and hope that throughout the rest of my life I have the continued grace to see opportunities to build these kinds of relationships and help all feel that they belong, no matter what.

Another person who comes to mind is a young student who was designated male at birth but who identified as female. She came from a very religious family who would not accept her as a woman. She came to school each day and changed into the clothing she felt comfortable in; as a school, we sought to make her feel welcome and protected. Everyone treated her with respect and love, especially knowing the challenges she faced at home. When she was old enough to move out, the guidance counselor and I ensured she had a safe place to go and helped ensure she graduated so she could go on with her life beyond school.

I mention these stories because they illustrate that students need to feel safe before they can learn. When they feel like they belong, we strengthen their ability to feel empowered and further develop their sense of self. Later in this book, you will read about how traditional assessment practices and testing greatly diminish how students feel about themselves and their willingness to even participate in learning. Educational institutions have an obligation to develop students not only academically but also emotionally and socially; we can do that by ensuring a sense of belonging in the relationships we develop. The vignette that follows describes the experience of Jessica Cimini-Samuels, a middle school science teacher in New York City, in creating a safe place for students.

Forming an LGBTQ+ Student Alliance

Several years ago in our staff meetings, we began to have frequent discussions about how we were meeting the needs of our "subgroups" of students, both academically and emotionally. We would discuss different racial groups, students with IEPs, the "bottom third," and low-income students. I was always the voice at the table saying, "And our LGBTQ students!" Everyone would nod and agree. Then we would continue the conversation around all of our subgroups except the LGBTQ students. They were such a mixed group academically, racially, economically, and emotionally that no one really knew where to begin. We all knew we had students that were coming out and many others that were still figuring out their sexuality and identity. But no one knew the best way to support these students.

I thought and thought about what I could do, and finally decided that we needed to give these students a safe space and a voice. I wanted to provide them with a place where they could feel comfortable being themselves and where they could find other students that were going through similar life experiences. I wanted to show them that our building was filled with allies and was a place that would love and accept them, so in September I approached my administrators about starting an LGBTQ+ Student Alliance. They approved, and up went the rainbow posters. In October we had our first meeting, and it was a huge success. We would start each meeting with a time for sharing, and early in our meetings, one student shared that she was happy to know she wasn't alone. That made it all worth it. I wanted all of my beautiful Rainbow Warriors to know that they were seen, accepted, and loved. The LGBTQ+ Student Alliance has been a huge step to making that happen.

In the months since starting the club, I have noticed a shift in school culture. The most important change is that students that are LGBTQ+ seem to feel more comfortable expressing their sexuality to teachers and other students. At the midpoint of the year, a student told the club that though he had publicly identified as female previously, he was ready to identify as male to the school community. We were able to have open and frank conversations about his transition. Other adults in the building felt comfortable talking to the student about it, and when they didn't, they would talk to me. The students in the club told me that other students would ask them questions about the club that were curious but respectful. There was an open dialogue happening, which is exactly what I had hoped for. Change and acceptance are happening in our school community, allowing our LGBTQ+ students to feel supported and accepted, which has also spilled over into the way they participate and engage in class. Developing a truly accepting community where students feel they belong allows them to bring their whole selves to their learning. Teachers with this knowledge also have an opportunity to adjust their assessments based on what they know of these students, ensuring that language is inclusive and assessment design doesn't unintentionally cause harm.

—Jessica Cimini-Samuels, middle school science teacher and LGBTQ+ Student Alliance advisor at Marsh Avenue Expeditionary Learning School, Staten Island, New York

Final Thoughts

Entire books have been written about the importance of developing relationships in schools and the impact those relationships have on learning. Because assessment is an essential component of learning, it makes sense that this book's focus on developing better assessment practices that consider the whole child should begin with a discussion of relationship building.

Relationships lay the groundwork for how we develop learning spaces. Simply put, if we don't take the time to build the various essential relationships that make schools tick, then we greatly hinder our ability to do our jobs well, regardless of which role we have—student, teacher, leader, parent/caregiver, advocate, and so on. In building these important relationships, we will learn what success means for individual students. Knowing what they require to be successful and how best to address areas in need of improvement will enable us to develop more effective and personalized assessments. We should be aiming for students to develop mastery in the skills related to our courses as well as the content they will need as building blocks for future learning. The more developed our relationships are, the more willing students will be to share challenges, take risks, and engage with their own learning, eliminating fear as an impediment because they know we have their best interests in our hearts.

Reflection Questions

1. How do I develop meaningful, trusting relationships with students?
2. How do I nurture student relationships to foster a culture of belonging and social awareness?
3. How do my own learning preferences contribute to the way I teach?
4. What structures do I have in place to develop connections with families and communities?

2

Developing Self-Awareness in the Context of Assessment

The learning and assessment experiences that students have in the classroom are a major influence on their self-awareness, affecting how they see themselves not only as learners but also as individuals in the larger world. CASEL (2020) defines *self-awareness* as follows:

> The abilities to understand one's own emotions, thoughts, and values and how they influence behavior across contexts. This includes capacities to recognize one's strengths and limitations with a well-grounded sense of confidence and purpose.

As educators, we must ensure that students aren't overly focused on grades and therefore drawing the wrong conclusions about themselves. We must make sure that they first clearly understand the expectations and learning objectives, then understand the progressive levels of mastery for those objectives, and most important, can identify which level they are on without our telling them.

This chapter addresses steps for explicitly teaching students how to identify their learning strengths and challenges and express how that awareness makes them feel. It considers how to help them set goals about what they learn, understanding that having a growth mindset means that they can accomplish anything with the right tools, help, support, and practice. It then looks at teaching the practice of reflection and how it both helps students to develop self-awareness and promotes better self-assessment. In addition, it explores learning dispositions and how student awareness of them develops better learning identities. Ultimately, when students display this kind of understanding, we can provide better feedback and instruction, and they can better advocate for themselves throughout the process.

Identifying Strengths and Challenges Through Formative Feedback

Misconceptions about formative and summative learning practices are common. Too often we put all of the weight of learning on the summative displays and too little on the process of getting there—the formative process. Formative practice is how learning is revealed. It is the opportunity we have to see how students are doing and provide the necessary feedback for better practice and learning.

Because formative work is often ungraded (and should be), students can develop a misunderstanding that it doesn't "count." But formative work is where the learning happens, so of course it "counts." As we develop our classroom learning environments, students need to trust that this is where they will start to identify what they do well and where they need to improve.

Project-based learning with a formative component is a great way for students to work in groups and individually. They have the opportunity to participate in a workshop environment with a full-class minilesson followed by time to work and get feedback along the way. As the teacher, this is your opportunity to do a broad check-in with each student to determine level of learning and to encourage and respond to questions. Because early on you worked so hard to develop relationships both directly with the students and among the students themselves (as discussed in Chapter 1), all of them should feel confident that their voices are valued. The goal is to provide equitable opportunities for help during class, so maintaining a record of whom you speak with and for how long will ensure that no one child monopolizes your time. If students appear to need more help than you can provide in a few minutes, you may need to do some direct instruction, either in a small group or individually at a different time. (See Chapter 3 for more on project-based learning.)

Developing Formative Tasks to Assess Individual Skills or Content Knowledge

When you design a particular project or notice students experiencing challenges more broadly, you should develop specific formative tasks that are short but address those challenges. These tasks should be aligned with a particular standard or content. They should have clear directions, and students should be able to do them multiple times. Ideally, you will co-construct success criteria with students so they know if they are successful doing the task. You can use the criteria for peer reviews, providing some sentence stems to gather useful feedback.

Figure 2.1 is an example of what that could look like from the work I do with the Core Collaborative (www.thecorecollaborative.com), based on Paul Bloomberg and Barb Pitchford's book *Leading Impact Teams* (2017). The school I was working with is Nicotra Early College Charter School in New York. Note the simplicity and clarity of the task's directions, its alignment to the reading standard (which is the same as the task), and how the prompt can be changed for ease of student practice. In other words, the teacher can use the same task about making claims with a different text, simply adjusting the prompt to suit the new reading. Some students may be able to show proficiency or even mastery on the first try, whereas others may need to make multiple attempts completing the same task with a different text. When using a holistic rubric like this one, the point is to break the standard down into a task and then only look for demonstration of the specific skills or other criteria outlined in the rubric. Teachers need to make sure *not* to assess anything that isn't part of the specific criteria on this task.

Unlike predesigned 4-point scaled rubrics, which often don't support students' growth, this formative task also provides teachers with a means for providing personalized feedback to students: teachers can collect data and provide specific feedback in the "Notes/feedback" sections of the rubric.

FIGURE 2.1

Holistic Rubric

HOLISTIC RUBRIC R1 Task Revised

Task: Using the following prompt, write a claim that demonstrates your ability to cite evidence, make inferences to support your analysis, and develop questions for deeper understanding.

Prompt: In the poem "Still I Rise" by Maya Angelou, whom is the narrator speaking for?

ADVANCED

- ❑ All the proficient criteria plus
- ❑ Determines where the text is **ambiguous.** (Where does it have a double meaning, or can it have more than one interpretation?)
- ❑ There's evidence of questioning for deeper understanding.
- ❑ Can connect to other texts besides the one provided.

PROFICIENT

- ❑ States a claim.
- ❑ Cites evidence that supports your claim.
- ❑ Supports evidence with analysis and explicit inferences that directly illustrate what the evidence is stating.
- ❑ Supports evidence with analysis and implicit inferences that clearly demonstrate **your own conclusion and opinion** about the evidence.

CLOSE TO/Approaching

- ❑ 3 of the 4 proficient criteria

Notes/feedback:

PROGRESSING

- ❑ 2 of the 4 proficient criteria

Notes/feedback:

EMERGING

- ❑ 1 of the 4 proficient criteria

Notes/feedback:

When using skill-specific tasks, first make your students aware of necessary new vocabulary and explore exemplars for what successful learning looks like around these skills. Providing authentic examples from other students will help your students connect to the learning and give them a realistic understanding of what their work could look like. Often, in my earlier days of teaching, I would create an example, sometimes overreaching and creating more anxiety for students because they didn't feel they could do the work at the level of the example I was sharing. Depending on the entry point of your students, make sure you show them several examples that are appropriate for their learning levels so they can see where they fit on the progression scale without feeling bad about their ability to learn.

Figure 2.2 is an example of an upper-elementary math rubric created by educational consultant Lori Cook. Note how it breaks down success in a way that students can understand and that would be easy for a teacher to assess and provide feedback based on.

Co-constructing Success Criteria from Standards-Aligned Rubrics

Once students understand the task and the progression through the various levels of proficiency, you can look at the criteria on the rubric together and determine what success looks like. You can begin by modeling the process and then working with students to determine what they need to do to be successful in each component of the rubric. Although the process may feel a bit repetitive the first few times you try, once students get into the routine, you'll see the benefits.

Including students in the process allows you to reemphasize the vocabulary they need to know to be articulate about their learning; it allows you to continue to promote a growth mindset (as described in the next section). As you help individual students understand where they are and then provide pathways for them to get to the next level, they improve their self-awareness and begin to develop an ability to advocate for their own needs.

FIGURE 2.2

Problem-Solving Response Rubric

ADVANCED
- All proficient criteria plus
- Provides multiple strategies and/or use of tools
- Explains how the multiple strategies support the solution

PROFICIENT
Claim
- Answers problem in context
- Includes units/labels in visual models and answers

Evidence
- Shows all work
- Includes visual models of the problem

Reasoning
- Explains why each strategy was used
- Uses appropriate math vocabulary
- Justifies why the solution makes sense (connects to reasonable answer)

CLOSE TO
- 5–6 of the 7 proficient criteria

PROGRESSING
- 3–4 of the 7 proficient criteria

EMERGING
- 1–2 of the 7 proficient criteria

Source: Courtesy Lori Cook. Used with permission.

Figure 2.3, which relates to the holistic rubric in Figure 2.1, is an example of what co-constructed success criteria could look like, with space for students' self-analysis of the status of their learning. Remember, the criteria should be expressed in student-friendly language, as shown by the "I can" statements in the figure. Students can then check the boxes

FIGURE 2.3

Form for Student Self-Analysis on Success Criteria

Success Criteria	Need Help	Got It	I Can Help a Peer
I can state a claim.			
I can cite evidence that supports my claim.			
I can support my evidence with analysis and explicit inferences that directly illustrate what the evidence is stating.			
I can support my evidence with analysis and implicit inferences that clearly demonstrate **my own conclusion and opinion** about the evidence.			

that indicate where they are in their learning. If they need help, they can go to a knowledgeable peer or to you.

Co-constructing success criteria with students makes expectations clear, which reduces students' anxiety about what they need to know and do—and, more important, how to be successful at it. Learning doesn't come easily to all students. Therefore, the more mystery we can remove from our expectations, the more students can feel confident about the learning we are asking them to do.

Helping Students Develop a Growth Mindset

Carol Dweck (2006) has done extensive research on growth mindset versus fixed mindset. Traditional school systems have supported the idea of a fixed mindset, often labeling students in one way or another throughout their learning experiences. Students quickly develop a notion about whether or not they are "good" at something and easily disengage or develop bad feelings and even anxiety around particular content areas that they have been "taught" they can't do. As educators, we have a responsibility to remind all students that they are capable. Some skills may be harder to learn and may require more practice, but if students are willing to do the work, they can achieve the goal.

Spending time in class discussing misconceptions about learning and giving students a platform to address concerns privately and as a group are ways to ensure a more positive self-concept around subject areas. After all, if you want students to *be* successful, you have to first remind them that they *can* be. When you hear students using language that aligns with a fixed mindset—for example, "I can't"—politely and gently remind them that they *can* and provide them with strategic feedback to assist in that goal. This feedback can come via small-group minilessons or direct instruction, personalized written feedback, one-to-one conferences, or peer review followed by teacher intervention.

In addition, remember that the language you use around learning matters. Be intentional about how you discuss new learning, and provide ample opportunities for practice and redos, downplaying the possibility of better grades and instead focusing on the need to work through new learning multiple times in multiple ways to increase efficacy. Avoid competitive language, and remind students that they are capable if they *do* the work. Partner with them to develop a plan, and then provide continual feedback, making sure to acknowledge and validate progress.

You can also share the research about growth mindset and assign reflection activities to help students confront how they see themselves as learners and start setting goals for moving past fixed beliefs. These kinds of conversations take time and can be supplemented with a daily reminder about how learning and mastering new skills requires time and practice. You can remind them that they didn't learn to ride a bike in one day, and so they certainly won't learn complicated math processes or foreign language skills in one day either. Good writing requires multiple drafts and revisions; scientific understanding requires exploration and time to deepen understanding. It is essential to give students these opportunities.

One last thing to remember is that we all have moments when we experience a fixed mindset; helping students understand when this is happening will be integral to their ability to name it, reflect on why they are feeling stuck, and then take action to shift back into a growth mindset. My father always reminds me that it is OK to feel down for a little while about something not going our way, as long as we don't get trapped in "stinkin' thinking." Remind students that they can feel disappointed or frustrated when they struggle, but a way out of such feelings is to remember that they haven't "gotten it *yet*." Patience, practice, and intentional steps will help them get back on track.

Helping Students Transfer Dispositional Skills Throughout the School Day

Making students aware of specific characteristics of successful learners can be an important part of helping them develop a growth mindset. What kind of behaviors do successful students engage in? How can we teach students to practice such behaviors and incorporate them into their sense of themselves? One way to do so is through the power of "learning dispositions" that relate directly to academic, social, and emotional growth. In the following vignette, Paul Bloomberg, author and CEO of the Core Collaborative, explains what learning dispositions are and how we can cultivate productive dispositions in our students.

Learning Dispositions: The *What* and the *Why*

The term *learning dispositions,* often called *habits of mind* or *dispositions of learning,* refers to the way in which learners (adults and students) engage in and relate to the process of learning. Guy Claxton (2018), author of *The Learning Power Approach,* describes learning dispositions as the foundation for the three kinds of learning going on in classrooms related to state and national standards:

1. Knowledge and conceptual understanding are being accumulated.
2. Skills and strategies are being developed.
3. Attitudes about learning and habits of mind are being developed.

Costa and Kallick (2008) list 16 habits of mind derived from studies of successful, efficient problem solvers from many walks of life. You can learn more about the 16 habits of mind by visiting their website, www. habitsofmindinstitute.org.

Various standards documents related to content areas actually incorporate learning dispositions. For example, the Common Core's Standards for Mathematical Practices and the Next Generation Science Standards (NGSS) Science and Engineering Practices are content-focused dispositions. The state of Texas has standards called "process standards." In addition, the Next Generation English Language Arts standards in New York State now include lifelong habits of a reader and writer. Such practice or process standards are vital for understanding and making sense of the content. The simple truth is, there is more to successful learning than content alone. Here are examples that illustrate the link between habits of mind and various content-related standards:

- Habits of Mind
  - Persisting
  - Taking responsible risks
  - Thinking flexibly
- Standards of Mathematical Practice
  - Persevere in solving problems
  - Attend to precision
  - Construct viable arguments
- NGSS Science and Engineering Practices
  - Constructing explanations and designing solutions
  - Engaging in arguments from evidence
  - Asking questions and defining problems

Cobb and Krownapple (2019) introduced the Dignity Framework for Educational Equity in their book *Belonging Through a Culture of*

Dignity. The Dignity Framework is grounded in four dignity competencies or dispositions:

- Patience
- Openness
- Listening
- Empathy

Cobb and Krownapple (2019) describe the importance of nurturing these dispositions in ourselves, because we can't give to others what we may lack. These four dignity dispositions must be unpacked for clarity and modeled for students by the adults in the building, and then we can teach and infuse these dispositions into our daily work alongside students. The goal is to create a learning culture in which students and adults feel validated, accepted, fairly treated, and appreciated.

Keep in mind that equitable practices and policies must be in place to ensure that our students are loved and cherished for who they are. Learning dispositions can be used as a weapon to oppress and label students. For example, if we see that a student prizes humor as one of their main learning dispositions, but we don't value humor or find it useful in our class, we can use this knowledge to belittle the student, making them feel worse about something they felt strongly about—clearly not the way dispositions should be used. It is best to assume that our students have successfully developed certain dispositions in some area of their lives, and so we would want to help them transfer that success to an area that they wish to improve. For example, when I was a music student, I could easily persevere through a challenging concerto I was working on, but when it came to geometry, I would just give up. Looking back, I can attribute my lack of perseverance to the fact that the teacher did not accept me or believe that I could do it. If he had talked with my music teacher, he would have seen that I had been persevering successfully through challenges for years with my music studies, and I just needed a bridge to connect the disposition.

Claxton (2018) explains that the positive or negative attitudes students or adults have about themselves as learners often have a direct effect on their overall learner identity and their learning outcomes. An unhealthy learning identity can detract from their ability to learn successfully, especially when they are put in challenging situations. Many students can demonstrate their knowledge and skills with fluency but cannot access that learning when they are required to transfer it for problem solving. Keep in mind, too, that learning identity and the related dispositions are contextualized. A learner may have a healthy learning identity in language arts but a negative identity in science or social studies.

A negative learning identity is reinforced through nonequitable practices and policies that make students feel dismissed, marginalized, or mistreated. An example is traditional grading, which doesn't give students the feedback they need to close the gap between failure and success. For example, when I was in high school, my perception that I was horrible in math was reinforced daily in class through the grades I received on pop quizzes, assignments, and unit tests. I never really understood why the teacher was grading me when I was in the process of learning something new. Then, to make matters worse, grades from my early learning through my development of more expertise would be averaged, inaccurately reflecting the improvement over time. There is no way to feel successful in this context. I was literally punished for making mistakes when I was learning something new.

It's likely that there are students in your school right now who feel like failures because they are working within a system that sorts and labels them based on their grades. To this day, I don't understand the reasoning behind it. My math learning identity was so unhealthy that I changed majors so I wouldn't have to take a statistics class. My negative learning identity functioned as a gatekeeper. I held myself back from endless opportunities because of an unhealthy attitude that started to plague me in geometry class. The good news is, I actually became a math teacher in an effort to overcome that negative learning identity. When I had to teach others math, my whole world changed. I realized, through a lot of reflection, that I could be good at math if I was taught conceptually and if my mistakes weren't used against me. If my teachers had tuned into my learning dispositions and had a better understanding of how I needed to learn, I would have felt more positive about my own math experiences. In the end, my own bad experience helped me provide less judgmental learning experiences for my students.

If our goal is to teach students to be resilient, lifelong learners who can solve problems and move through the challenges of life and work, cultivating core learning dispositions in our students is essential. They need to be reflective and self-aware so they know how to activate the dispositions needed and access the related intellectual patterns of thinking so they can persist through challenge.

We can create buy-in and ownership with students by inviting them into the design process, co-constructing competencies for core learning dispositions. When students are a part of the design process, they learn how successful people think, act, and feel. Co-designing dispositional learning experiences is vital for the level of transfer needed for success in K–12 schooling, higher education, life, and career. The goal is threefold:

1. We want our students to hone their abilities to be more self-aware.
2. We want them to determine what disposition(s) are needed for success.
3. We want them to be able to activate those dispositions and their related intellectual patterns of thinking so they can move through any challenge that stands in their way.

—Dr. Paul Bloomberg, CEO, Core Collaborative,
and coauthor of Leading Impact Teams *and* Peer Power

One way to help students understand learning dispositions is to have them brainstorm what a person would be feeling, saying, or doing if they had activated a certain disposition in a challenging situation. You could extend this exercise by having students write scripts based on short scenarios in which they must activate different dispositions. These activities help deepen students' understanding of themselves and others as learners.

The best way to implement learning dispositions is to infuse a few of them throughout a school. Begin by including students in the decision about which dispositions to focus on. This kind of schoolwide decision, with student involvement, leads to cohesion throughout the school day, promoting community and coping skills wherever students go and helping them develop a positive attitude about themselves as learners.

Motivating Students Through Goal Setting

Often, educators insist that students are motivated by grades, but I would counter that they are motivated by reaching goals. Teaching students to set academic and social-emotional goals that develop their personal dispositions in a positive way will help motivate them in their work and also encourage them to prioritize and simplify what they are working on at any given time. Actionable goals provide opportunities for them to measure their progress and take ownership of their learning, and for you to be supportive of their choices.

In addition to class goals that you may set based on specific content you are teaching, individual students may need to be working on particular skill sets or content knowledge. Most likely they will know that they need help, based on feedback from you or their peers indicating that they aren't quite meeting the standard yet.

Obviously, the complexity of the goals will depend on grade level: goals for young children are less complex than those for older children. Isaac Wells, assistant director of professional learning with the Core Collaborative, shares how we can get even our youngest students to set learning goals. In Chapter 8 of *Peer Power* (Bloomberg, Pitchford, & Vandas, 2019, pp. 123–136), he outlines the steps for supporting goal setting with primary students learning to read, but the steps are applicable to other areas as well:

1. Establish clear success criteria. ("What will it look like when I am successful?")
2. Communicate and connect the criteria to actions. ("What do I need to do to be successful?")
3. Gather evidence and provide feedback. ("What evidence supports the criteria, and what feedback would assist with goals?")
4. Set personal goals. ("What do I want to be able to do?")
5. Self-monitor and reflect. ("How am I doing? How have I improved? What will I do next?")

Read on for more discussion on goal setting from Isaac Wells.

Developing Children's Goal-Setting Skills

We know that at a very young age, children set and work toward achieving goals. They want to make themselves understood, and so they learn to cry when they want something, then to smile, and eventually to talk. As they get older, if they want something out of reach, they learn to roll, scoot, crawl, and, later, walk. They have the motivation, they usually have a strong support system, and they are always clear on what they want the end result to be.

What children experience in school often contrasts with this seemingly natural ability to maintain focus, persevere through repeated (and often painful) failures, and find their own way. However, we can encourage and accelerate learning in reading, writing, number sense, problem solving, and other areas when we structure the learning process to match their natural curiosity.

Without the innate drive that children have for something such as learning to walk, the first step is often simply to make them aware of the goal. All learners, but especially those in the primary grades, need to be aware of both the end goal and the steps along the way to master the skills and understanding.

"Big" goals can be difficult for young children to understand when there are no clear steps along the way. For instance, "I will learn to tie my shoes all by myself" is a great goal, but it's really all or nothing. By contrast, the goal "I will learn to say all the letters in my name" can be broken down into a first step ("I will learn the first letter in my name") and then build from there. Similarly, learning a certain number of high-frequency words or counting to 5 or 10 allows students to measure progress along the way to mastery. All of these examples, including "tying my shoes," have two attributes that are essential to developing goal setting early on: (1) they are concrete, and (2) the steps to achieving them can be observed. Students receive feedback from themselves as they compare their current ability to models of success. Teachers clarify the next steps with feedback that might include comparing examples, modeling, or simply having a conversation meant to help the child recognize what needs to be done next.

We want children to see that the benefit of setting a goal is in accomplishing something and being able to celebrate that accomplishment. When you draw attention to students' successes and help them to see how they made progress toward their goals, they come to understand how their efforts can affect their learning.

You can track students' progress using checklists, index cards, or spreadsheets, but the point is, students need to see their progress. For many goals, portfolios of student work or photos of what they have accomplished allow them to look back and see how they have progressed. In some cases, it makes more sense for students to represent their progress in another way, such as moving an avatar across a chart in their goal folder or having their initials added to a chart that shows how many books they have read or how high they can count accurately. Even small indicators can have a powerful motivational effect when children recognize they are making progress toward their goal.

Revisiting the earlier list of steps for supporting children's goal setting, we can imagine the following teacher-student dialogue:

1. Establish clear success criteria.
   Teacher: "This is how we count to 10 using dots."

2. Communicate and connect the criteria to actions.
   Teacher: "Look and listen to me say each number as I slide the dot into the group."

3. Gather evidence and provide feedback.
   Teacher: "I see that you are able to count up to 4 using the dots. You are being careful to say only one number as you move each dot."

4. Set personal goals.
   Student: "I want to count to 10 using the dots. First, I have to be able to count to 5 on my own."

5. Self-monitor and reflect.
   Student: "I have been practicing, and now I can count to 6 using the dots! If I'm not careful, I forget what number I'm on, so I have to say one number for each dot."

After this initial process, a sixth step might consist of revisiting a current goal or setting a new one, checking in again on a product or conducting another observation to gather feedback, or even continuing to self-monitor and reflect. The one nonnegotiable is that students have an opportunity to continue the learning and practice until they are successful. If they feel the learning is "over" because the lesson is over or a grade is given, they are likely to stop regardless of where they are in relation to their goal.

Grades—or their approximations in the form of check marks, plus signs, smiley faces, or stickers for a job well done—may serve as rewards for young children, but they do not motivate students to learn. Learning requires reflection, revisiting, rethinking, and revising. When children understand what the end result will be and see a clear path toward success, they choose to come back to the work again and again, engaging in a process that is no different from what they do when they play. Whether they are trying to build the tallest block tower, make it across the monkey bars, or read a more challenging book, the goal, not the grade, motivates the learning.

—Isaac Wells, assistant director of professional learning, Core Collaborative

Learners in middle school and high school can set goals based on the written or oral feedback you have provided. They can track their progress against specific skills they are working on based on that feedback, start making their own decisions about personal goals, and advocate for help in achieving them. As described in the next section, students can reflect on their progress toward achieving their goals, and you can then use this information to better facilitate learning for students through continued conversations about achieved goals and where to work next.

Teaching Students to Reflect on Learning

After students have set goals and participated in learning experiences, they need opportunities to review their work and their process so they can reflect effectively. Being a "reflective person" is different from reflecting on learning in a productive way. Reflecting is an academic disposition as well as a core part of being self-aware. It is important to teach kids explicitly what you mean by reflection and explain the reasons for doing it. You need to ensure that when you say "reflection" to your students, everyone has the same understanding of what is expected.

Beyond merely identifying what reflection is, you need to explicitly help students recognize next steps that will allow them to move beyond what they notice. Once they can articulate struggles and successes, you need to get them to ask, "Now what?" What do these struggles reveal about themselves as learners, and how do they develop perseverance to push through what doesn't come naturally to them? How can they go even further and "reflect on their reflections"?

To get students to reflect effectively, you must first scaffold the process of how to do it (a topic I discuss at length in my book *Teaching Students to Self-Assess* [Sackstein, 2015b]). Much like a short formative task with a rubric and success criteria, reflection needs to be taught, practiced, and evaluated with specific feedback. In my experience, most students understand that reflection includes identifying what they have learned to some degree, but they often mistake reflection as an opportunity to share what they did and didn't like about the learning experience. This sharing isn't inherently bad, but it isn't what I'm talking about here. Students need to write reflections that (1) state what they understood the task was asking them to do, aligned with expectations; (2) describe how they completed the task; and (3) express how they believe they did on the task, based on the standards being assessed. Using evidence from their own learning, they should demonstrate an understanding of what they have learned and how. The third part is the one they will need the most feedback on. Figure 2.4 is an example of a successful reflection written by a high school senior.

In the next student example (Figure 2.5, p. 48), note the personal struggle the student experienced but also how she talked herself into working through the task. I wouldn't have had that insight had she not written this reflection, and it gave me an opportunity to view her work through the lens she provided. The feedback I could then give her was more specific to the challenges she had.

FIGURE 2.4

Student Reflection for an Analysis Paper

We were asked to select a poem from a list of approved poets given to us and create a thesis statement around some kind of poetic device. We had to analyze and interpret the poem in our own way and write a paper on it. Anne Bradstreet was one of the first authors I searched online and I thought that her Puritan background and the way she was shunned from having materialistic wealth in her life was interesting, so I chose to write a paper about one of her poems. I began reading the list of poems she wrote and her poem "The Vanity of All Worldly Things" was the one that caught my eye the most, so I read the poem and chose it as my poem for my analysis paper.

One challenge I faced was writing about *how* the author means what she means instead of *what* the author means. I knew what my poem meant, but I just didn't know how she meant it. After reading the poem over and over, I decided to focus on two elements: diction and structure. That way, I could focus on how the author means [what she means] through her use of diction and structure in the poem. For example, I wrote how Bradstreet uses diction and structure to exhibit the vanity that everyone and everything displays in their endless journey to become the best, which is my thesis of my essay. I then wrote how Bradstreet uses a variety of blissful diction such as "honor," "wealth," "satiates," "beauty," "vain," "fame," "pleasure," "wisdom," "youth," "conceit," and "immortal" throughout the poem to show that people are ignorant because they relate vanity to all things glamorous, whereas in reality, vanity is an evil that is deadly and destructive. Also, I added that Bradstreet lists words such as "pearl," "gold," "crystal," "sapphire," "onyx," and "topaz" to illustrate the idea that the world is vain and is full of objects to fulfill the people's vain desires.

Another challenge I faced was organizing my ideas on my analysis paper, but thanks to peer editing in class, Michelle was the person responsible for focusing on organization in the essay so she helped me a great deal.

One standard I met was "Evaluates the draft for clarity of focus, progression of ideas, development, organization, and appropriateness of conclusion in order to identify areas requiring further invention and research." I met this standard because I had to constantly revise and edit my drafts of my analysis paper in order to develop more ideas, organize them, and improve them until my analysis paper was perfect in the final draft phase. We also had to bring 4 copies of our second draft and have our peers edit them for clarity, organization, and any errors that were in the analysis paper. My drafts of my analysis paper showed that I revised them over time and how I developed my ideas and organized them.

Another standard I met was "Selects a topic, identifies what he or she knows about the topic, and determines the need for additional information." I selected the poem that I wanted to analyze for my paper, but I had trouble writing about how the author means what she means, so I decided to obtain additional information about the author of the poem [that] would help me. After learning [about] Bradstreet's Puritan background and how she was shunned from materialistic wealth, I decided to tie her background into the fact that Bradstreet's Puritan background was evident in her use of materialistic diction since she used it to symbolize the materials as being one of the causes of people's annihilation. Also, with Bradstreet's dramatization of the main problem of living in the world without becoming worldly, she advises the readers that it would be best for them to avoid materialistic wealth just like how she shunned them from her life.

One way I would improve my analysis paper is to add another element to talk about how the author means what she means besides diction and structure. Also, I would improve my analysis paper by adding more in the conclusion since it looks a bit short.

Source: Courtesy Monica Sharma. Used with permission.

FIGURE 2.5

Student Reflection for a Paper on *The Great Gatsby*

So for this paper, we had to choose a question from a list of questions that were provided to us, and from there we had to write a 3–5-page essay . . . yay . . . not really. Anyway, the question was based off of the book *The Great Gatsby* by F. Scott Fitzgerald, which was actually a really good book, in my opinion. Writing this essay was not very enjoyable, though. The very task of writing this essay was so strenuous to my mind, soul, and body that . . . OK, that may sound a bit dramatic, but in all honesty, I had the hardest time with this essay compared to all the others. I keep telling myself, this will pay off, it just has to pay off, and it's my motivation to keep going. Optimistic much? Well, what else can I be when I'm sitting in front of the computer staring at a blank screen for hours? To pass that time I did research on the time period, but somehow most of the things I found were not really relevant or what I was looking for. I finally came to the conclusion that trying to write about the time period itself might be a good place to start and might get the essay and my thoughts flowing. I found that it actually worked, but there was still an issue with stringing my ideas together. I felt that I had the right ideas, but they weren't really con-nected. Did I mention that this is, like, the hardest essay that I've had to write? I don't know why, but for some reason it was.

I decided to be late. Though I could have finished my essay just in time, I felt turning in what I had would be a complete waste for you to read. Honestly, I didn't like it, but at the same time, I didn't hate it. I liked some parts of it, but it just didn't really connect at certain parts, and I also just felt that it wasn't good enough. Miss Sackstein, if it isn't good enough for me, I refuse to turn it in. I know it may sound ridiculous, or maybe you do understand, but I'd rather turn it in late and take the grade deduction knowing I did my absolute best instead of turning it in on time knowing I could have done better. I feel like I did a better job with this paper than the previous one, but that could just be my own opinion . . . hopefully I did.

I felt that I met all of the following standards: W1.1 Student analyzes components of purpose, goals, audience, and genre. W2.1 Student takes inventory of what he or she knows and needs to know. W2.2 Student generates, selects, connects, and organizes information and ideas. W3.1 Student generates text to develop points within the preliminary organizational structure. W3.2 Student makes stylistic choices with language to achieve intended effects. W4.1 Student evaluates drafted text for development, organization, and focus. W4.2 Student evaluates drafted text to determine the effectiveness of stylistic choices. W5.1 Student edits for conventions of standard written English and usage. W5.2 Student employs proofreading strategies and consults resources to correct errors in spelling, capitalization, and punctuation. W5.3 Student edits for accuracy of citation and proper use of publishing guidelines. W5.4 Student prepares text for presentation/publication. Though I felt I met all these standards, the ones I felt I did best on were W3.2, W4.1, W4.2, W5.1, W5.2, W5.3, and W5.4.

Source: Courtesy Abigail Bogle. Used with permission.

Also note at the end of her reflection that she mentions a lot of standards but doesn't specifically address how she met them, as the student in the previous example does. It would be my responsibility to provide feedback about how she could point to evidence from her paper to support what she is suggesting in the standards section. In addition, I would probably set up an in-person conference to discuss her struggles and see if we could jointly come up with some helpful strategies for the future. A conference would not only deepen my relationship with her but also provide valuable insight about why she found the assessment challenging, so that I could perhaps differentiate the assignment in the future.

The goal of reflection is that students can speak to their learning in an articulate and specific way, addressing the goals they have set, describing the strategies they have employed, and then discussing how successful they were and why. This kind of information will lead to optimal data collection, enabling you to provide feedback that will enhance current and future learning. It will also help you develop future assessments that honor student voice and that give you the information you need to help individual students progress at a pace that is appropriate for them.

Of course, there is more than one way to reflect, and it would be unfair to suggest that written reflection is more effective than other forms. Whenever we prize written modes of learning over others, we perpetuate *graphocentricism,* which can function as a form of white supremacy in education. In his article "Biases of the Ear and Eye," Daniel Chandler (1995) explains:

> The bias in which writing is privileged over speech has been called graphocentrism or scriptism. In many literate cultures, text has a higher status than speech: written language is often seen as the standard. Until the early twentieth century, linguists tended to accord priority to written language over speech: grammatical rules were based on written language and everyday speech was largely ignored; the prescriptive tradition was based on the written word.

Because of this bias, we should offer students other ways to share their ideas about learning—for example, an illustration, a video, or an audio recording, based on what best suits them. The ultimate goal is to make sure they know how to discuss what they are learning and why, and where they need continued work. How they communicate this information is less important than making sure that they communicate it at all.

Regardless of form, reflection is a skill with lifelong benefits, as evidenced by these comments from three former students of mine. Melissa Iachetta, who is now an on-site project supervisor and GIS (Geographic Information Systems) technician III, said this:

> I think self-reflecting and having to talk about and articulate my work has helped me tremendously later in life. It actually is a big part of why I am now the supervisor of a team of 12 people! I am able to manage because of what you taught me. The skills in learning how to point out patterns, have a critical eye for people's work, and deduce ideas from that are invaluable in management. I've actually had employees commend my reviews and say that they actually feel like they got tangible

feedback that they can use for improvement. I think I am good at a pro-and-con balance in reviewing people and seeing where they need work but also where they excel. That helps me delegate work that needs to be done, so these skills help on so many levels.

Fourth grade teacher Jenna Schiffman offered this observation:

Writing reflections around my work enabled me to be in control of my own learning and think reflectively, which are skills that I need to use on a daily basis as a teacher. Additionally, I learned to support my opinions and ideas with specific evidence and proof.

And Barbara Kasomenakis, a recent graduate of Skidmore College, said this:

Reflection writing allowed me to watch my own thinking process and shape the next iteration of similar learning experiences. Yet it was not until [later that] I understood that the act of even asking students to reflect would make the most lasting impact on me. When teachers or professors acknowledge their students' thoughts and discoveries, there is a sense that we are learning from one another. This transfer of learning from educators with obviously more background in their respective fields communicates respect and reciprocity to students, something often over-looked by institutions who regard their student body as a monolith. By fostering this transfer of learning, I was able to advocate for myself, make hypotheses and self-discoveries about learning, and feel more inclined to ask for help from seemingly intimidating pedagogues!

There is no better way to understand the impact of our teaching than speaking with current and former students and hearing their thoughts. We just need to listen.

Encouraging Students to Be Self-Advocates

Ultimately, we want students to leave school with the ability to advocate for their own needs. A huge part of achieving that goal is first teaching them to identify their strengths and the areas where they need help, as discussed earlier. The relationships we build with them will strengthen their own resolve, and they will learn to ask better questions so that they can get the help they actually need.

Assessment is all about understanding what students know and can do and then taking that information to adjust our curriculum and develop more targeted learning experiences that help them continue to grow. When students can successfully self-advocate, we have a working partnership that allows them to deeply connect with their own needs and feel more confident as learners.

You can invite older students to self-advocate by encouraging them to sign up for one-on-one conversations during designated office hours. Having these dialogues outside of class time allows you to give the student your full attention. For younger students, one-on-one conversations can happen before or after the school day, or at the beginning or end of specials. You don't want to take students away from classes they enjoy, but you also don't want to spend precious class time with any one student, especially in a high school class, which may have more than 30 students.

As you teach students to self-advocate and give them opportunities to do so, it is important to be cognizant of who is responding to the offer and who is not. If you note that certain students need help but aren't taking advantage of these opportunities—perhaps students who have been conditioned to think they don't matter or that they "aren't smart enough"—offer an alternative that both honors their dignity and helps them learn to amplify their own voices. For example, you might require all students to make an appointment to meet with you during office hours. This way, no one is singled out, and the students who need help get it. You can also use this private one-on-one time to coach them through the act of asking for help when they need it to destigmatize the effort. All children have a right to get the attention and help they need. Spending your time equitably should include trying to accommodate students and meeting them where they are. Too often, students don't take full advantage of extra help or don't know how to self-advocate. Whatever the reason, it's important to create an environment in which help doesn't feel like punishment and isn't offered or forced upon students in a way that fails to respect what they have to offer in the conversation. Creating an environment in which students can articulate their needs gives them a chance to be empowered and successful.

Two former students and now college graduates, Alyssa Striano and Zachary Damasco, offered their views on their experiences related to self-advocacy and its connection to reflection. Alyssa had this to say:

> Reflections definitely helped me learn to self-advocate beyond your classroom because they made me aware of my capabilities from a more honest, unbiased perspective. Through reflection, I have been able to be real with myself and recognize what is my best work and what may not have been my best work, which was something I wasn't so aware of pre-reflection. Knowing when something of mine is actually strong helps me to respectfully stand up for myself if I notice that something is unjust, as I can look at what I've done and give specific reasons to defend my thoughts.

Zachary described a somewhat different experience:

> So personally, I don't feel the reflection process made me more willing to advocate for myself (I say that because, reflection process or not, my personality type was always comfortable with defending my work if necessary), but it did make me more confident when backing my position. The key to this was how the standards weren't finite and provided the opportunity for an outside-the-box approach in order to satisfy/exceed them. Concurrently, you were a teacher open to accepting unorthodox work, which allowed that self-advocacy to flourish. In my opinion, the flexibility of the standards' definition paired with the openness of the grader to accept potentially unconventional arguments are both essential to making students more willing to self-advocate. If the standards are too strict, or the teacher is too strict, you fall into the same boat where a student will just do the work to get it done because it won't matter if they can back up their work if no one will listen to them . . . something I and pretty much every student has experienced at one time or another.

Final Thoughts

Self-awareness—knowing ourselves as human beings and learners—is an essential part of personal development. The better we know ourselves, the more we are able to make good decisions and to navigate both positive and challenging experiences that can steer the direction of our lives.

Giving students the tools of self-awareness and then listening to what they share promotes equity in our learning spaces. Each child's learning experience is different and therefore requires us to provide something a little different in our teaching and other interactions. The more opportunities we provide for students to share how they feel about learning and where they are struggling, and to advocate for themselves, the better they will become at doing so. Developing self-awareness can improve not only how they approach their learning in the future but also their sense of self-efficacy.

Reflection Questions

1. How do I contribute to an atmosphere that encourages self-awareness, including self-advocacy?
2. How do I model reflection to encourage the practice in my students?
3. What goals am I working on, and how am I making them visible?
4. What challenges me about developing robust formative assessments that encourage the strengths of my students?
5. What role do my students play in developing success criteria?

3

Facilitating Self-Management
for Better Learning

One of the biggest frustrations that teachers at all levels endure is related to student self-management and regulation. Whether it's time management, organization, classroom connectedness (i.e., how students choose to fit or connect or choose not to), or behavioral challenges, we have all struggled with students who have issues in these areas.

CASEL (2020) defines *self-management* as follows:

> The abilities to manage one's emotions, thoughts, and behaviors effectively in different situations and to achieve goals and aspirations. This includes the capacities to delay gratification, manage stress, and feel motivation and agency to accomplish personal and collective goals.

Think about how these skills manifest in your learning spaces. What if your students were specifically taught self-management in a variety of situations, and instead of being chastised for not doing it well all of the time, learned various strategies for overcoming their challenges?

In addition to their general usefulness, self-management skills can help high-anxiety students who become easily overwhelmed and have difficulty compartmentalizing—for example, students who do well in class and then struggle on high-stakes assessments. Explicitly teaching self-management skills can boost students' confidence and increase their ability to be successful.

It is important to note that, within the context of the SEL framework developed by CASEL, the competency of self-management has come under criticism in terms of how it pertains to students of color:

Schools, like most other U.S. social institutions, tend to prioritize prevailing middle-class, American culture. Student success requires acculturation, or at least a familiarity with American core cultural meanings, norms, and practices. For low-income youth and immigrant youth, this can induce acculturative stress, which occurs when youth encounter a cultural mismatch between the expectations and norms of their host (e.g., U.S.) and their home (heritage). Such stress has been associated with a number of mental health problems and maladaptive behaviors among the U.S. and immigrant-origin youth.

Discrimination experiences are related to but distinct from acculturative stress. Discrimination refers to the perception of unfair treatment or the subordination of an identifiable social group. Racial/ethnic discrimination has a number of interpersonal and institutional manifestations and is a common experience for people of color. Experiencing discrimination is associated with a host of negative socioemotional health outcomes. Importantly, reactionary and self-defeating responses to cultural and racialized stress and micro-aggressions often result in punishment of students of color. (Jagers et al., 2018, pp. 5–6.)

In this chapter, we explore ways to facilitate the development of self-management skills and organize students' learning both in and out of the classroom. Having well-developed relationships with students before you start working on these skills, including being attentive to cultural considerations, will help you determine the best approach without creating harm. The ultimate goal is to empower students to take ownership of their learning.

Time Management

Time management is a struggle for some students, adolescents in particular. It becomes more essential as students get older, with fewer people reminding them when things are due and learning occurring in different places. Perhaps it was easier in elementary school, where they may have spent most of the day in one classroom, with one teacher who stated expectations explicitly. Switching classes in middle school can reveal new concerns about time management and the need to develop this skill.

It is not enough to remind students to write things down in their agenda books or to organize areas of their notebooks, folders, lockers, or digital drives. Many students may be unresponsive to such efforts because, as noted in a book I coauthored with Connie Hamilton, "it's . . . likely that those students just don't know how to keep track of assignments or manage time because nobody has ever taught them those life skills" (Sackstein & Hamilton, 2016, pp. 39–40). And so we need to provide specific structures and methods that teach students how to do these things well and help them understand the positive impact that self-management will have on them both now and in the future.

At the same time, it's important to remember that "there isn't a one-size-fits-all solution to getting kids organized and developing their sense of responsibility. Each student might need a little something different to help him/her move toward becoming an independent learner" (Sackstein & Hamilton, 2016, p. 39). Fortunately, there are many things you can do to help students develop this muscle—or at least help them become more aware of their strengths and challenges with time management.

Calendars and Agenda Books

Among the many high- and low-tech tools that you can teach students to use, the most important starting point is a calendar. For visual learners in particular, having space on a calendar where they can write down what they have to do—and even plan backward for how much time they need—provides a framework for sorting out their time.

Many schools provide students with agenda books that include both the school handbook and a calendar. The calendar has month and week views, with space for each class. Providing class time for students to write down assignments and other information in the calendar is one way to help them get in the habit of doing so, especially for those who seem to be less inclined to remember to do it on their own. You can also post a reminder on the board or elsewhere in the classroom. Of course, getting students to write down information in the calendar is only part of the process; you also have to get them in the habit of actually referring to it.

Learning how to use a calendar or planner is a skill that even elementary students can develop, with your help. At this level, "planners are often used as a diary of the day's events. Students copy a sentence or two off the board as a way to communicate from school to home what happened today or a reminder for what to bring tomorrow" (Sackstein & Hamilton, 2016, p. 40). But you can expand the use of planners to encourage additional habits. Here are some suggestions:

> Instead of using a planner to exclusively document each day's events, model how a detailed calendar helps them to plan. When you send home a monthly calendar, ask students to enter the events into their planners, getting help from parents if needed. Encourage them to add family activities as well; this will create a complete picture of what a student needs to plan around for his/her time. In class, regularly prompt students to look forward in their planners to consider what they have coming up in their schedules. Perhaps a favorite aunt has a birthday next week—the student might choose to use this event as the theme for a poem about the aunt as a gift. Teaching students to plan ahead will reduce procrastination and highlight the benefits of thinking about how to manage time instead of watching it fly by unproductively. (Sackstein & Hamilton, 2016, p. 40)

For older students, providing copies of a class syllabus that highlights important dates makes it easier for them to plan long-term goals related to their learning. You can offer further support by demonstrating how to use the reminder function in apps such as Google Calendar:

> As they enter due dates, students can determine how much notice they need in advance. Some students might send themselves a "get started" reminder message while others would benefit from "project is due in 3 days." This personalized approach to teaching them how to manage time honors individual students' work habits in a way they won't feel nagged but still have beneficial reminders. (Sackstein & Hamilton, 2016, p. 41)

Assignment Timelines and Benchmarks

When you develop a project or an assignment that can't be completed within one class period, it is often a good idea to divide it into smaller parts, with benchmarks indicating when students need to submit each part along the way to completion. This approach has some key advantages: giving students smaller tasks that build up to the larger product makes the work more manageable, and you can review the students' work at successive stages of the process, provide specific feedback, and catch students who may be going astray before it is too late.

Figure 3.1 is an example from one of my classes of what an assignment sheet could look like for an extended project or paper. Note the

---

FIGURE 3.1

Assignment Sheet for a Final Research Paper

Overview

Students will write a 12- to 15-page paper (typed and doubled-spaced) addressing two or more literary texts read this year through a particular critical theory lens.

Objective

To teach students how to research, write, and source an academic paper to ready them for college. Students will learn how to use a college library to aid in the completion of this assignment.

Topic specifics

- Select two or more pieces of literature read this year. You may compare/contrast/analyze theme, style, diction, or other literary devices or elements.
- Select a particular critical theory to discuss or to analyze your chosen work (for example, formalism, structuralism, reader-response criticism, psychoanalytic theory, Marxist criticism, new historicism, feminist literary criticism and gender studies, biographical criticism).

(continued)

FIGURE 3.1

Assignment Sheet for a Final Research Paper (*continued*)

Paper specification

Paper will be 12–15 pages long, with page numbers centered on the bottom, double-spaced, 1-inch margins, Times New Roman, 12-point font.

- The paper should have a title.
- Research should be done on your thesis. What have others said?
- Research should be done on your authors and on your critical theories.
- Works cited and works consulted pages *must* be included (annotated bibliography).
- Proper MLA citation throughout the paper is *required*.
- A 2–3-page reflection that charts your progress and process must be attached (more on this later).
- All intermediary work (copies of articles, notes, ideas, etc.) must be included.

Intermediary check-ins and conferences/expectations

You will be required to conference with me at least one time while you do your research. In this conference, you will be expected to show me your research and preliminary writing. You should also come with specific questions and challenges you are facing.

We will be doing informal check-ins several times a week in class. Your work should be with you at all times, as we will be working on these papers every day in class until they are due.

Assessing for this paper

You will be getting feedback based on individual standards on this paper using the same standards as before from the AP rubric and AP standards found on the College Board's website.

Mastery achieved: Has a clear thesis that addresses at least two pieces of literature through a critical literary theory lens, develops ideas fully, research is evident (but not overwhelming), in-text MLA citing is correct, a "works cited and works consulted" page is present. The paper is organized well, with coherent and appropriate transitions. The writing is clean, sophisticated, and stylized with few mechanical errors. There should be a clear conclusion. All work is attached.

Proficiency achieved: Has a clear thesis that addresses at least two pieces of literature through a critical literary theory lens, develops ideas adequately, research is evident (but not overwhelming), citing is correct, "works cited and works consulted" page is present. The paper is organized but has some transitional issues. The writing has some mechanical errors. There is a conclusion. All work is attached.

Approaching proficiency: Has a thesis that addresses at least two pieces of literature through a critical literary theory lens but does so with only a surface understanding, develops ideas but not completely, research is evident (but not overwhelming), citing is attempted, "works cited and works consulted" page is present. The paper is organized but has some transitional issues. The writing has mechanical errors. There is a conclusion. All work is attached.

Emerging, not there yet: Has a thesis that addresses at least one piece of literature through a critical literary theory lens but does so in a way that indicates limited or no understanding, ideas are mentioned but not fleshed out appropriately, citing is attempted, "works cited and works consulted" page is present. The paper is organized but has some transitional issues. The writing has mechanical errors. There is a conclusion. All work is attached.

No research paper will be accepted without preliminary work or a "works cited and works consulted" page. If you need additional support with these things, please set up a conference for help.

Reflection on the process

As you work through this process, I'd like you to keep careful notes about what you are doing. What kinds of challenges do you face? How do you solve them? What steps do you take?

After the fact, you will reflect on the work you have done. Did it go as you planned? What went well? How do you know? What would you need to do it differently?

Benchmark dates

- 5/5—Working topics for research paper due
- 5/6—First trip to Queens College (QC) library
- 5/10—Working thesis statements due
- 5/11—Plan of action due
- 5/12—Second trip to QC library
- 5/13—Annotated bibliography due (works consulted/cited using Diigo.com or something you're more comfortable with)
- 5/16—Outline due
- 5/17—Third trip to QC library
- 5/19—First draft of paper due (at least five pages typed and double-spaced)
- 5/23—Conference during college library day (list to be e-mailed beforehand)
- 5/25—Second draft due (8–10 pages typed)
- 6/6—Final research paper due (hard copy and electronic)
- 6/6—Reflection due—paper uploaded to e-portfolio

level of depth and detail provided to ensure that students are clear on the expectations and specific due dates. During this project, I kept a spreadsheet that allowed me to check off when students submitted their benchmark work, especially if they were submitting it before the deadlines. The spreadsheet also gave me a place to take notes during our check-ins and conferences and helped me keep tabs on the students who were struggling with the load or expectations, prompting me to engage with them more often. Because my goal was for all students to be successful, I also spent time with them discussing what they were doing to keep up and what their main challenges were. If it was apparent that they simply worked more slowly than other students, there was no need to offer suggestions. But if they indicated an organizational or time challenge, such as procrastinating or being easily distracted, we worked out potentially helpful strategies.

For short, in-class assignments, you can help to ensure that students complete the work on time by writing checkpoints on the board and then activating a fun sound to indicate when time is up for completing that particular segment. For group work, students can develop their own benchmarks for completing the assignment. Checking in with students periodically while learning is happening in class is also helpful.

Project-Based Learning

Project-based learning (PBL) is "a teaching method in which students learn by actively engaging in real-world and personally meaningful projects" (https://www.pblworks.org/what-is-pbl). It is not project-based *assessment*, which involves assigning a project that students work on primarily outside class and then submit when they're finished. Instead, it supports classroom teaching by promoting authentic learning experiences that require students to dive deeply into inquiry tasks that are of interest to them. Project-based learning is a great way to help students develop self-management skills (as well as all the other core SEL competencies) while building essential academic skills and content knowledge.

In his book *Rigorous PBL by Design*, Michael McDowell (2017) discusses how designing excellent PBL allows students to deepen their surface-level understanding of content and ultimately transfer their knowledge. Rather than using traditional methods for teaching and then assessing with quizzes and tests, PBL engages students and allows you to really see what kids know and can do *throughout* the process, because continual feedback and problem solving are built into the structure. Pointing out the potential benefits of a problem-based approach, McDowell describes PBL as "a pedagogical vehicle that . . . could meet . . . 21st century outcomes, mimic work-related actions of the 21st century, and give students the opportunity to solve real-world problems in real time" (p. 145).

Beyond offering students an opportunity to solve real problems, you can allow them to *choose* the problems they want to address. These might include service-learning opportunities that can help students develop civic awareness and social skills. In her article about using PBL as a tool for social justice, educator and PBL advocate Charity Moran Parsons (2018) discusses how project-based learning can help students dive deeply into social justice issues that are important to them:

> Throughout . . . a project's path, . . . we can continue to leverage the students' questions, ideas, and concerns about the matter at hand. As students work to formulate their answers to the driving question, we can provide opportunities for students to reflect upon the questions they began with, any answers they may have uncovered, and any new questions they may discover. (para. 9)

Citing Tabitha Dell'Angelo (2014), Parsons notes how the constant referral back to students' original questions and ideas fulfills four recommendations for creating classrooms for social justice: (1) connecting to students' lives, (2) linking to real-world problems and multiple perspectives, (3) creating classroom community, and (4) including authentic assessments. She also acknowledges teachers' eagerness to suggest questions for students to consider, and urges that they instead allow students to take the lead:

> I love when teachers anticipate and plan for the questions they'd like students to explore and consider. I often ask teachers . . . What will you do to support the students' arriving at these questions on their own

(empowering them with voice and choice) as opposed to telling them that these are the questions they'll discover? I'm always also interested to see what questions the students themselves will generate! (para. 10)

As Parsons suggests, project-based learning is a fantastic way to incorporate student interests into the learning and assessment processes. As students work on their projects during class time, you can offer help as needed and give them hands-on experiences to develop skills and content that connect to their own lives. And because projects are done over an extended period of time, they provide ample opportunities for students to practice their time-management and goal-setting skills.

Research Papers

Like PBL, research papers take time, and allowing students to do much of the work in the classroom, with your support, increases their likelihood of success. Even for many adults, it takes years to become a competent researcher, so expecting our 4th graders or 9th graders to do it well without help is unrealistic. In terms of self-management, diving into the challenge of research definitely requires students to develop and display related skills, including managing stress and finding motivation— especially when the research isn't going well.

I often compare the steps involved in research to the steps leading to and including marriage. When students are first trying to decide on their topic, they are in the courting phase of a relationship. They may even be "dating" a few different ideas at once. As time passes, they consider whether or not their relationship with the topic is worth pursuing, and then they make a commitment to go deeper. As in all committed relationships, there is struggle. Their sources may not always support their original premise. They need to be flexible in how they respond to finding this new information and make continual decisions about their commitment to their topic based on what they learn. Being "married" to their topic means that they're all in. They understand that not every source is going to support what they need or offer a new path for digging deeper.

You may find that students who are doing research for the first time become easily frustrated with this process and may be tempted to quit prematurely. Your support for students should include having benchmarks within the assignment and modeling how to develop a topic and what to do when they don't find what they need or if they need to adjust their topic based on the information they have found.

Having students write a plan of action and an outline is an important first step in guiding them toward success. This activity gives students time to really think about what they want to say and do, as well as set personal benchmark dates and times for getting the work done and meeting project deadlines.

Figure 3.2 is an example of a student's plan of action and outline for a research project I assigned. The student submitted the plan and outline before handing in the first draft of her research paper. As a teacher, I had the opportunity to provide feedback at this early stage and let her know if she was on track and where she might want to add more depth before she even began writing.

For this assignment, I gave students the freedom to select their own topics, books, and critical lens through which to study the topic. In class, I gave them an overview of each lens, and I built in time for exploration in the college library. In addition, students were expected to complete an annotated bibliography before developing their outline so they could be sure that their topic had enough depth to explore.

Elementary students can write plans of action, too, although they would obviously be less detailed than the example in Figure 3.2. Teachers can model for students what they want them to do by helping them create plans of action together, backward planning from the end product.

Regardless of grade level, make sure students have ample time when doing these in-depth assignments. Again, plan for them to do most of the work in class or in a library together. Depending on their age, students should be expected to do only a moderate amount of lifting at home. Remember, the goal is to help students be as successful as they can be without dumbing down the work or doing it for them. Provide

---

FIGURE 3.2

Student's Plan of Action and Outline for a Research Paper

Plan of Action

1. Write a detailed outline of what I am going to talk about in my essay, so when I begin to write I have a clear template of what I'm doing. (Friday and Saturday)
2. Do more research on Orwell to get myself situated and know what I'm going to try to prove. (Saturday)
3. Begin writing my introduction—starting big like we were taught in class (big ideas in the introduction and then narrowing into the topic). (Sunday)
4. Write my first draft, focusing on what I already know about my books and my topic without providing quotes or any direct information. (Monday)
5. Try to find Bloom's Guide on *1984* at Queens College and other books that show Orwell's view on war; maybe go back to the books that I originally had and take a closer look. (Wednesday)
6. Once I have gathered all my research, maybe search up more sources using the internet and then begin to add more to my first draft to create my second draft. (Wednesday)
7. Peer review with people doing a similar topic and/or meet with Ms. Sackstein if I need help.
8. Make corrections to my paper and perfect it.
9. Organize my bibliography.
10. Get all my work together and hand in.

Outline

I. Introduction
   A. *Big idea*—We are influenced by everything and everyone that we encounter through the course of our lives, which can have from minuscule to life-changing impacts on our lives. When these influences come, unexpectedly, the struggles that one faces in trying to adjust can blur the lines of what we thought was right and wrong.
   B. *Context*—O'Brien's *The Things They Carried* follows a group of men during the Vietnam War. These men, although conscious of their choice to go to war, were shocked by the events that they encountered, and in the midst of processing their horrifying experiences and attempting to effectively deal with them, they began to change their view on everything. Orwell's classic *1984* is about Winston Smith, a man caught in the oppressive society of a nation called Oceania. After living in a place where you cannot trust anyone, you are always being watched, and there is no "past," one would think that there would be a sense of conformity and these would seem like the norm. But to

Winston, this life didn't seem right, and eventually, his frustration got a level past discomfort, leading him to view the entity of Big Brother and the society as a whole differently.

C. *Thesis*—George Orwell's *1984* and Tim O'Brien's *The Things They Carried* demonstrate the effects of war and an oppressive government on one's beliefs, through flawed and at times deeply traumatized characters, indicating the author's stylistic choices as a reflection of their views on society and politics.

D. *Transition to next paragraph*

II. Talk about wars/oppressive governments and their effects.
   A. Natural rights and what could happen if they are taken away.
   B. Living through war or in a society that is constantly in a war mindset can make this life seem like the norm, but when taken out of such society and exposed to the opposite (or vice-versa—coming from an opposite society and being exposed to this) can mess with people's ability to process things, leading them to rely on sometimes dangerous coping mechanisms.
   C. What war is (in my opinion) and why living in a state of war or oppression is not good and can lead to changes.

III. Text 1: *The Things They Carried*
   A. The Vietnam War and the mindset during this era, how it affected people.
   B. How the things they carried proves my thesis: O'Brien's *The Things They Carried* clearly shows this throughout the novel from very small details like the things each man carried (coping mechanisms) to events that demonstrate a shift or growth in a character.
   C. Try to make a connection between the characters from this novel and outside sources like *Generation Kill*, a Showtime series based on a true story. Look at how a fictional character like Lieutenant Cross is so much like the real Sergeant Colbert and try to do the same with other major characters from the novel, like Tim, to showcase how accurate the novel is in portraying real effects of war, and Azar to Lance Corporal Harold James Trombley, as well as Rat Kiley and Corporal Josh Ray Person.

IV. Text 2: *1984*
   A. World War II and the Cold War and how it affected the mindset of people during this era and how it changed society as a whole.
   B. Oppressive society: Forbidden to write in diaries, thoughtcrimes are the worst types of crimes, children are conditioned to love Big Brother more than their parents to the extent that they would be able to report their parents, changes made to the language to prevent a rebellion, people disappearing and people not allowed to question change.

(continued)

   C. How the frustration from the oppression opens Winston's eyes to the wrongs in his society and pushes him to take risks that are life-threatening, like meeting with a girl, buying and writing in a diary, trying to find evidence against Big Brother, and much more that leads him to being held captive.

V. O'Brien
   A. How the Vietnam War relates to O'Brien and his views on war; also why he wanted to write this novel to show how close he is to this novel and maybe make the connection that parts and people in this novel are a reflection of himself.
   B. How his stylistic choices are a reflection of his views—look at the things he has said and the way he feels about certain things and see how it is illustrated or mimicked in the novel by characters. Try to focus on Tim, the lieutenant, or another major character as well as major parts in the novel.

VI. Orwell
   A. His connection to WWII and the Cold War and why he felt the need to write *1984* as well as his view on war and oppression, in general, to make the connection that Winston is a reflection of himself.
   B. Point out his stylistic choices such as the whole format of this society (the concept of Big Brother, the rules, the extent of oppression) and compare it to the way his life was or how he pictured it to be like (or feared) after the Cold War to make the point that *1984* is essentially a book of his views on society (or criticism) during this time period.

VII. Add something else to further prove my point—maybe compare both novels or mention another novel (*Cat's Cradle*) as an outside source to reinforce my theme OR mention other books written by these authors and how they do the same thing in those books as well (ex: Orwell—*Animal Farm*).

VIII. Conclusion:
   A. End big: Something on the basis of circumstances that can be related back to the theme of this essay (war) and psychology.
   B. Leave the reader thinking: Make a point or propose a question that everyone can connect to, maybe mention something that everyone experiences and how that too can be viewed through the same lens.

Source: Courtesy Ardhys De Leon. Used with permission.

structures that allow them to chart a course but also to have enough freedom to creatively approach their research.

Mindfulness

Mindfulness coach Charlie Anstadt defines mindfulness as "presently knowing what you are doing or being fully aware of the present moment." The point of being mindful is to not worry about all of the potential challenges or outcomes in a situation, but to stay focused on what is right in front of us, within our control.

Modeling and teaching students how to use mindfulness in the classroom can help them regulate their anxiety and stress about assessments. In many schools, high-stakes testing promotes the most anxiety among students because of its role in determining how successful they will be and what kind of opportunities they will have in the future, based on the results. My intent here is not to discuss the merit of such testing, but to acknowledge that it does happen and will likely continue in varying forms for the foreseeable future, prompting an obligation to ensure that students can handle the situation.

Of course, mindfulness is not a miracle cure that will work for all students all of the time, but you can offer it as a tool for students who really struggle to stay focused or who forget what they know when they are nervous. You can teach simple breathing techniques to help them relax before an important test. These techniques will help slow their heart rates and promote a calm that will help them stay focused. Here are two that Charlie Anstadt recommends:

- **The Check-In:** Invite students to sit upright in their seats, gently close their eyes, and focus on their breathing for 10 breaths, in and out. While they do this, make sure they are aware of their posture but are relaxed. They should recognize the various thoughts that may come to mind but let them go as quickly as they came in. At the end of the 10 breaths, express the intention of being fully present for the task at hand.

- **The Body Scan:** Start with the check-in but stay focused on the breaths. While the students are focusing on their breaths, draw their attention to their feet and direct them to relax that part of their body. From there, continue upward until they get to their head, all the while focusing first and then relaxing after drawing their attention to the specific body part or area. This exercise is designed to connect students to their bodies and the present moment, which will decrease anxiety about outside issues.

In a review of the literature on mindfulness as it relates to education, in an article titled "Mindfulness and Student Success," Matt Leland (2015) lists potential benefits: "minimizing the impact of bullying, helping students with learning disabilities, benefiting students who are training in careers with high emotion and stress, and coaching" (p. 19). According to Leland, "students who have mindfulness incorporated in their curriculum could potentially reap benefits academically and personally" (p. 19).

The article addresses areas where mindfulness is particularly helpful, starting with academic performance and the acquisition of learning skills. Focus is central to being able to learn well, and practicing mindfulness keeps students focused so they can dive deeper into critical-thinking tasks.

In addition to its potential impact on academic concerns, mindfulness, with its emphasis on personal awareness of the present moment, can help with behavioral issues and control of emotions. It can de-escalate emotional situations and help to reduce bullying in schools. When we teach kids how to think about their breathing and to understand their own emotional states, and then teach them strategies for coping with and working through challenging moments, everyone benefits. In addition, students are better able to express what underlies their initial emotional reactions.

Leland advocates for teaching mindfulness across age levels and subject areas, from physical education to math. If students come to understand the value of presence of mind and body while they are learning or competing or playing or working, they will become more adept and connected to the learning.

As educators, we can and should model this behavior. I'm not saying you have to go to yoga classes or meditate in groups. (To be honest, I've never really gotten into yoga, although I've tried many times. Breathing in bent-over or twisted positions with my head near someone else's behind just didn't leave me feeling very relaxed.) For me, mindfulness is being present with my thoughts. I go for walks or runs; sometimes I ride my bike. I pay attention to my breathing when I start to get upset about things. I even have the words "practice patience" tattooed on my arm. The better we can model being present and mindful for our students, the more we can enjoy being in our shared space. Personally, I have found that practicing mindfulness with my students (and by myself) has been an integral way to keep myself patient, focused, and emotionally grounded.

When I started teaching, I was too busy to slow down and take account of my emotions (or so I thought), and I almost burned out very early in my career. I wish I had had the skills then that I have now. Just being aware of my frustrations and having strategies to deal with them has helped immensely, which is why I started teaching those skills to my students as well. The more we can help them be in touch with and deal with their spectrum of feelings, the better able they will be to function when the feelings arise.

All this being said, mindfulness doesn't necessarily function the same way for all people, and although we think we are doing right by our students by asking them to engage in mindfulness activities to help with their self-regulation, we may inadvertently trigger them instead. In an interview with Mindful.org, Dr. Angela Rose Black of Mindfulness for the People (a Black-owned social change agency that offers culturally responsive mindfulness trainings) noted,

> [T]here is an overt assumption [in mindfulness curricula grounded in whiteness] that the content presented is universally beneficial to EVERYbody. That the empirical evidence driving the curricula is "robust and rigorous" so *of course* its application is relevant to EVERYbody. And all of this universality is assumed while never having to say that decades

of evidence-based, well-funded, highly visible, and industry standard findings that support mindfulness curricula and practices are predominantly normed on the lived experiences of White people. (*Mindful* Staff, 2017, para. 5)

Thus, if we are going to use mindfulness as a way to help students stay emotionally healthy and focused, we need to recognize that, if led by a white teacher, it may not be effective for all students—indeed, it may alienate students of color—and shouldn't be forced on those who don't feel inclined toward it. We need to allow students to use methods that work for them. We can also work with colleagues to create alternative opportunities for students who may need a different leader for this activity.

Stress Management

Students can exhibit high anxiety or an inability to focus in class whether or not the learning is high-stakes. Those suffering through panic attacks or other anxiety disorders are not going to do their best work. It helps to know which students struggle with this issue and to have a system in place that doesn't shame them but provides a way for them to manage their stress and keep being productive. The overall goal is to create a safe and flexible classroom environment that can adapt to various situations.

Using Counselors and Social Workers

Guidance counselors and social workers (when available) are a valuable resource that many teachers underuse. If you have students who become easily agitated, work with the counselor or social worker to develop a protocol that enables students to leave class to calm down. At one of the schools where I taught in New York City, I developed a close relationship with our guidance counselors and social workers. The social worker I worked with allowed me to send individual students to her as needed, and I had an agreement with the students that they would complete their learning when they were ready, without any penalty. Teachers who don't have this kind of arrangement with school counselors or whose schools have limited resources should talk to administration about designating a go-to person for this purpose or coming up with a creative solution. Perhaps you could set aside a quiet space in an office where students can go in times of need and adults can arrange to check in to make sure students are OK.

As a parent of an anxious student, I have felt reassured that he had the ability to leave class upon request to visit his counselor. He never abused this privilege, but used it to calm himself when he got too angry or upset in class—a situation that often happened with teachers with whom he didn't have good relationships.

Being Flexible About Group Work and Independent Work

We know that some students like to work independently, and others are naturally more collaborative and prefer to work with their peers. Either way, students can become anxious when the work format is not what they prefer. Although we should find a way to accommodate both kinds of students, we should also require them to stretch—to learn the skills that don't come naturally. After all, there will be times in life when they will be expected to collaborate and other times when they will be expected to be independent.

To ensure that students are developing the skills they need and are also having their social and emotional needs met, aim to create a classroom environment that offers multiple opportunities for both independent and group work. Often, I created group projects to be done in class while we were exploring literature and new skills associated with the texts. Students would work together to problem-solve and build the skills. These projects were not graded. I asked the students to reflect on what the group had learned and then to apply that learning to an independent assignment that they also reflected on afterward.

The independent assignment offered the opportunity for summative assessment. Although students didn't receive a grade on this assignment either, they were assessed against standards and their level of mastery on the standards. They had multiple opportunities to revise as needed if they chose to review the feedback provided and make further corrections and revisions. This iterative process took some of the anxiety out of a formal assessment because students knew they would have multiple opportunities to practice the skills and then demonstrate their knowledge.

For more on the advantages of combining individual and group work in the classroom, read the following account by Zak Cohen, an educator who has lived and taught in Morocco, China, South Africa, and the United States.

Flexible Grouping: Collaboration Reimagined

At 62 years old, my mother-in-law went back to school at the University of Minnesota. She was thrilled to be getting another degree and was excited about the courses she was taking—until halfway through her first semester, when she called me and my wife to complain about "yet another group project."

"Nobody else was prepared for our meeting! I ended up doing everything!" she exclaimed. "And I just don't understand why I have to work with people I hardly know."

She was vocalizing something that we have all felt at one point or another—frustration with group work. Of course, such challenges aren't limited to students; teachers struggle with group work as well.

Educator, blogger, and podcaster Jennifer Gonzalez recently posed a question on Twitter regarding the obstacles that teachers encounter when assigning group work. Unsurprisingly, clear trends emerged in the more than 130 replies, ranging from issues of student accountability and the uneven distribution of work to uncertainty around feedback protocols. Mainly, though, teachers expressed their frustration in composing balanced groups—a delicate and often tenuous exercise that has to account for academic standing, dispositional traits, and social-emotional compatibility.

Given the time-consuming task of forming groups, some educators confessed that they have altogether eliminated group work from their classes. While this response is somewhat understandable, eliminating group work isn't the answer. We know from countless studies that collaboration is one of the most important 21st century skills. So we must ask ourselves, "How can we preserve collaboration while reducing the headache of group work?"

For many teachers, the solution lies in having students select their own groups. However, there are many obvious downsides to this approach. It runs the risk of leaving some students on the sidelines searching for a group. It also doesn't necessarily best serve student learning, as students must work in lockstep with one another, irrespective of individual pace or preference. For example, if students have to read a passage for their project, completing this step as a group probably isn't the optimal approach. And yet, students don't have the option to work independently, even on a single part of their project.

In defense of this approach, some teachers argue that it mirrors collaboration in the real world, but that isn't totally truthful, is it? In a professional setting, we often have a choice about when to work independently and when to work collaboratively, and we make this choice depending on the task at hand. Since any given project comprises multiple discrete tasks—each of which requires different forms of collaboration—group work in the real world is often a dynamic, not static, process.

One way to authentically replicate real-world collaboration in the classroom is through a *flexible grouping model*. In a flexible grouping model, no assignment is explicitly independent or collaborative; instead, the balance is struck by the learners themselves. By factoring in task, pace, and level of challenge, students can work independently, with a partner, or in small groups. Within a single class period, multiple permutations may exist, as students make a new choice with every new instruction.

When students enter my classroom, the first thing they do is check to see where they left off in the last class. From there, they read the next instruction and make a decision about whether they want to work independently or collaboratively. Having made their choice, they signal it to their classmates with a paper cutout of either the number 1 or 2: students use the 1 to signal to their classmates that they would like to work independently; students use the 2 to signal to their classmates that they would like to work collaboratively.

The fluid, organic nature of this system has myriad advantages over the more static traditional model of group work:

1. **The development of metacognition and personal management skills.** Metacognition and personal management skills are essential in both school and the workplace. Flexible grouping helps to develop these skills, as students need to think about where they are in their learning, what the task demands, and how they learn best. Only when these questions are answered can students make a choice about whether to work independently or collaboratively. Over time, students begin to identify and refine their own best paths for accomplishing their work as they begin to become increasingly aware of who they are as a learner.

2. **Student-owned flexible learning spaces.** When students choose to work independently or collaboratively, they must also make a decision about *where* to work. In this way, individuals, partners, and small groups must manipulate the environment to optimize learning. Students make personal decisions about where to work and truly make the space their own.

3. **Peer experts.** With flexible grouping, expertise becomes a public resource. In my class, there's a list of skills I identify as being relevant to success on a given assignment. Over the course of their work on this assignment, students identify themselves as experts on one or more of these skills. Students who might be looking to collaborate can reference this chart and meet with a peer expert to engage in a conversation or run through a peer-editing protocol.

4. **Learning, not lethargy.** We know how powerful stasis can be, so students who start class working independently may be inclined to work independently for the entire class. For this reason, we have a saying in my class: "Learning, not lethargy." The decision making in flexible grouping is therefore not a one-off, but rather an ongoing series of decisions. Students must make continual

choices about whether to work independently, with a partner, or in a group, according to the instruction/task at hand, and not the project as a whole.

5. **Learning comes first.** When it comes to a traditional style of group work, students often have to deal with issues unrelated to their learning, including interpersonal relationships, absences, and groupthink. But with flexible grouping, the learning comes first. Students form and disband groups according to the task, so these issues are nullified.

6. **But learning isn't the only factor.** Especially in a middle school, we need to account for the social-emotional aspects of learning. Sometimes, students just need a little bit of alone time. In a flexible grouping model, students can work independently without drawing attention to themselves. For students who may be feeling a bit more social on a given day, they, too, can scratch this itch without disrupting learning. In this way, flexible grouping accounts for both introverts and extroverts.

When it comes to personalized learning, we've come a long way in allowing students choice in terms of the *what, where,* and *when* of their learning, but what are we doing to allow students choice when it comes to the *who?*

Source: From "Flexible Grouping: Collaboration Reimagined," by Z. Cohen, 2020, *The Core Collaborative blog.* © 2020 by Zak Cohen. Adapted with permission.

Other Strategies for Self-Management

Beyond time-management strategies, mindfulness techniques, and approaches to dealing with stress, there are several things you can do to help your students understand and develop various aspects of self-management. These include explicitly identifying characteristics of successful learners, using classroom jobs to encourage responsibility, sharing think-alouds to demonstrate accountability, and acknowledging responsible acts (Sackstein & Hamilton, 2016).

Identify characteristics of successful learners. Begin by asking your students to come up with examples of traits that characterize successful learners (for example, "likes to read," "follows directions," "is well organized") and write down their responses. Group the qualities into various categories, such as "knowledge," "responsibility," "attitude," and so on. Then, depending on the age of your students, create common definitions of these category labels. Good and bad examples of what different traits look like will further clarify definitions. This list could be displayed in the classroom, available as a reference throughout the school year. Some teachers even have their classes sign the list, as evidence that students will strive to personify these traits. If you have multiple classes, each group of students should create its own unique list of words.

Use classroom jobs to demonstrate responsibility. Many teachers post a job chart that describes things students can do to help manage the classroom. Assigning jobs to students has various benefits. It "not only helps you carry out your duties, but also provides students with a sense of purpose and daily responsibility that is visible in the classroom" (Sackstein & Hamilton, 2016, p. 42). The tasks should include a level of accountability such that failure to carry them out would be noticeable and consequential. An example would be gathering attendance data at the beginning of class. Having a class job involves another layer of responsibility if a student has a prearranged absence, which would require the student to find a replacement. The layers of responsibility involved in classroom jobs are visible to all students. They see "the impact of how important it is for the role to be filled and the effect it has on everyone if it's not" (Sackstein & Hamilton, 2016, p. 42).

Share think-alouds to demonstrate accountability. Think-alouds are a good way to model how students might consider possible consequences of situations or actions and plan for the best possible outcomes. Here's an example:

> I'm not going to be in class tomorrow. What responsibilities do I have that will not be taken care of if I'm not here? My class job this week

is the communicator, so I need to talk to the student substitute [a job from the work chart used in class] to have her fill in for me tomorrow. I'm also going to need to find out what I missed. I will alert the secretary to let him know I'll be touching base with him when I return to class the following day. Actually, if I text him after school tomorrow, maybe I can get the information tomorrow, finish it tomorrow night, and then I will be ready to learn and not behind when I get back the next day. (Sackstein & Hamilton, 2016, p. 42)

Acknowledge responsible acts. It's important to acknowledge students who implement your classroom norms. Such recognition should include contacting parents/caregivers to share specific examples of the responsible behavior. You might also ask parents/caregivers what they do to instill a sense of responsibility at home. If they have some good ideas, you can apply those strategies in the classroom. If they indicate they would welcome your help in this area, offer to partner with them and provide examples of how they can help their child further develop responsibility and time-management skills at home.

The Disconnect Between Homework and Self-Management

Accountability is an important component of self-management, as noted either explicitly or implicitly in other sections of this chapter. However, one area left unexplored so far is the controversial idea of using homework as a vehicle for helping students develop accountability.

Many teachers argue that homework teaches accountability. I strongly disagree. Homework creates all kinds of equity challenges and often hurts students who are already struggling. We simply can't have policies requiring daily homework that gets graded, with students accumulating zeroes for not submitting the work on time. We shouldn't penalize students if their accountability issues are related to poor self- and time-management skills—skills that we are in the process of teaching them to improve.

As a general rule, homework shouldn't exist in elementary schools. In an essay on research related to homework, Alfie Kohn (2012) supports that stance and discusses the issue more broadly:

> Let's start by reviewing what we know from earlier investigations. First, no research has ever found a benefit to assigning homework (of any kind or in any amount) in elementary school. In fact, there isn't even a positive *correlation* between, on the one hand, having younger children do some homework (vs. none), or more (vs. less), and, on the other hand, any measure of achievement. If we're making 12-year-olds, much less 5-year-olds, do homework, it's either because we're misinformed about what the evidence says or because we think kids ought to have to do homework *despite* what the evidence says.
>
> Second, even at the high school level, the research supporting homework hasn't been particularly persuasive. There does seem to be a correlation between homework and standardized test scores, but (a) it isn't strong, meaning that homework doesn't explain much of the variance in scores, (b) one prominent researcher, Timothy Keith, who did find a solid correlation, returned to the topic a decade later to enter more variables into the equation simultaneously, only to discover that the improved study showed that homework had no effect after all, and (c) at best we're only talking about a correlation—things that go together—without having proved that doing more homework *causes* test scores to go up. (Take 10 seconds to see if you can come up with other variables that might be driving both of these things.)
>
> Third, when homework is related to test scores, the connection tends to be strongest—or, actually, least tenuous—with math. If homework turns out to be unnecessary for students to succeed in that subject, it's probably unnecessary everywhere. (Kohn, 2012, paras. 2, 3, 4) (emphasis in original)

In addition to the lack of evidence supporting the value of homework, I would argue that homework takes away time that would be better spent on other activities. Kids need after-school time to decompress, engage with family members, and, most important, play. Unstructured play time is essential to child growth and development.

Final Thoughts

Each of us possesses strengths and challenges in our personal character. Teaching students self-management skills that can help them address their personal challenges, beginning at an early age, will set them up for success. Time management, organizational skills, and the ability to focus on tasks are among the competencies they will need both in and outside the classroom. That doesn't mean students won't have bad days, but having a variety of self-management strategies at hand can help them stay on track. Whether taking mindful breaths and putting challenges into perspective or breaking big tasks into manageable ones, students will have opportunities to turn negatives into positives—and then everyone wins.

If you face self-management challenges, be transparent with students and share your strategies. Let them know how you struggle or have struggled and how you got through it. Remember that relationships are at the heart of everything we do, and this is another opportunity to strengthen the ones you are building with your kids.

Reflection Questions

1. What kinds of opportunities do I provide for students to practice their time-management skills? What could I do better?
2. What are my own self-management strategies, and how can I model them in the classroom?
3. How do I manage time to prevent burnout in myself and my students?
4. How do I make decisions about group and independent work for the benefit of student learning?
5. How do I help students perform better on assessments and pace themselves through a learning experience?

Teaching Responsible Decision Making to Promote Student Ownership of Learning

Teaching responsible decision making is one way to promote student ownership of learning, giving students agency in how and what they are taught. Many students, particularly younger students and adolescents, often don't think through the consequences of their decisions. That shortcoming, although normal in terms of child development, contributes to their problems and challenges in school, which is why we need to ensure that students are aware of the consequences—both good and bad—of their choices.

CASEL (2020) defines *responsible decision making* as follows:

> The abilities to make caring and constructive choices about personal behavior and social interactions across diverse situations. This includes the capacities to consider ethical standards and safety concerns, and to evaluate the benefits and consequences of various actions for personal, social, and collective well-being.

When we think about this definition in terms of both formative and summative assessment, we further understand the need to weave the skill into our lessons. For example, if a student decides to skip class and misses important formative assessment activities, their learning will lag behind the expected level of mastery for the grade level, and they'll struggle to catch up. If a student decides to spend hours playing a video game after school instead of doing research related to their role in a group project, the entire group may suffer the consequences of a lower grade—and the student's relationships with peers may suffer as well. In addition to incorporating decision-making skills into our lessons, we must provide opportunities for students to take control of their learning and practice the skills through formative learning experiences. Too often, we assume that decision-making competencies are innate, a set of skills we are born with, but that isn't so. Whether we learn from what we see modeled (explicitly or not) or from our own experiences, being intentional about the decisions we make helps us have more control over our lives.

Imagine the benefits of helping students understand the consequences of potentially harmful actions before major damage happens. Such benefits might include saving them and their families considerable heartache and loss, as well as creating an atmosphere where better teaching and learning occur because students are actively involved in making good decisions about their learning both in and out of class. An environment that promotes student agency through better decision making enables students to express what they need (to be self-advocates, as discussed in Chapter 2) and thus to have more control over how they learn and are assessed.

Consider how many opportunities students have each day to make better decisions that can affect them and those around them in positive rather than negative ways. What choices will they make? In this chapter, we explore how we can both help students make better decisions and provide ample opportunities for them to reflect on those decisions and the resulting impact on their learning.

Moral and Ethical Choices

High-stakes assignments and assessments often put students in the position of having to make moral and ethical choices. As a deadline fast approaches, it might be tempting to decide at the last minute to plagiarize a published work, hoping not to get caught, or to "borrow" a friend's work and copy the whole thing verbatim instead of using it as a model.

When students resort to copying or plagiarizing, it's best to address the issue directly and help students understand the consequences. Beyond getting a zero, having to redo the work, or getting in trouble, students need to understand why choosing to take the easy way out hurts them and those around them. Feeling the emotional weight of making bad decisions contributes to better problem solving in the future. By getting students to reflect on why they made the choice they did, what the impact of that choice was, and how they can make a better decision to rectify the poor one, you reduce the likelihood that they will make this error of judgment again. Partnering with students to help them problem-solve in this way can also help you create environments where students see the value of learning and want to engage in a productive and ethical way, not just because it is required, but because they are invested in the learning.

You can help students understand the reasons for and consequences of a decision they made by doing a brainstorming exercise with them. Figure 4.1 shows an example of how such an exercise could be diagrammed. The central box shows the action that followed a student's

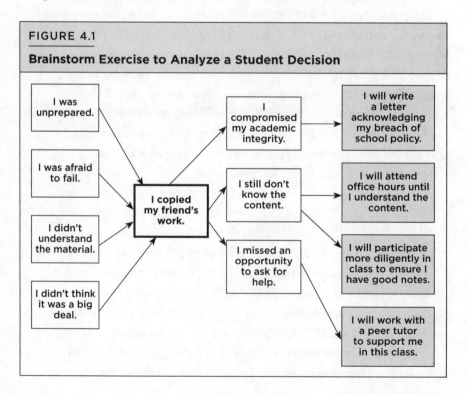

FIGURE 4.1

Brainstorm Exercise to Analyze a Student Decision

decision—in this case, "I copied my friend's work." (Other possibilities include "I cheated on a test" or "I cut class to avoid having to hand in a project that was due.") The boxes on the left represent possible reasons for the decision. The unshaded boxes to the right of the central box state the immediate consequences of the choice. The shaded boxes specify things the student could do to avoid making the same poor decision again. Teachers, school leaders, or guidance counselors can go through this process with students to help them make better choices in the future.

One way to minimize or even eliminate the temptation to copy or plagiarize is to build assessments around assignments that simply can't be completed by engaging in such behaviors. Assignments that involve multiple skills and tasks, such as projects that students are expected to do in class, with your support, reduce the likelihood that they will feel the need to appropriate outside sources to complete the work.

The Role of Collaboration

Collaborative environments in which students share ideas and develop understanding *together* can minimize individual students' negative decision making about their learning. Students have the capacity to significantly help one another, whether working through a problem set or providing feedback based on specific success criteria. When you allow these student-to-student relationships to thrive, you empower students to make responsible decisions *collectively.*

The establishment of study groups, buddy partnerships, and critical friends can be an effective way to support students' learning throughout a unit as well as to mitigate their concerns as they prepare for high-stakes assessments. Nurturing deep relationships among students will enable them to eventually self-select the people they can best work with for group assignments and projects in addition to test prep. They can reflect on their choices later, considering whether those choices were effective for learning or if they need to make adjustments in the future.

Environments that support student interaction include physical elements, such as seating areas around the room that invite collaboration.

When collaboration is part of classroom activity, students should feel like they have the agency to decide where they want to work and with whom.

Time-Management Decisions

As discussed in Chapter 3, time management is an important factor in student success, and helping students make better decisions about how they spend their time, especially as related to preparing for high-stakes tests, can lead to better outcomes. Part of making responsible choices is knowing the likely outcome of those choices. Such awareness can help students make the most beneficial choice (for example, using various methods, spread over time, to prepare for an exam) rather than the possibly more appealing choice (for example, spending time socializing with friends after school and postponing study until the night before an exam).

Of course, decisions related to test preparation require that you give students options for how to allot their time. You can offer to provide extra help at designated times or set up structures for peer tutoring well in advance of the test. You can make review sheets and videos available throughout the learning of the material—an approach that can make test prep less stressful because the students know they have helpful resources to increase their understanding.

Cultural Stereotypes and High-Stakes Assessment

Something to be aware of is "stereotype threat"—how certain cultural stereotypes can feed into both the anxiety and the performance of marginalized youth. An article written by the American Psychological Association (APA) discusses research on stereotype threat and how it can widen the achievement gap. Citing the work of psychologists Claude Steele and Joshua Aronson, the article relates the following account:

> Steele and Aronson gave Black and White college students a half-hour test using difficult items from the verbal Graduate Record Exam (GRE). In the stereotype-threat condition, they told students the test diagnosed intellectual ability, thus potentially eliciting the stereotype that Blacks

are less intelligent than Whites. In the no-stereotype-threat condition, the researchers told students that the test was a problem-solving lab task that said nothing about ability, presumably rendering stereo-types irrelevant. In the stereotype-threat condition, Blacks—who were matched with Whites in their group by SAT scores—did less well than Whites. In the no-stereotype-threat condition—in which the exact same test was described as a lab task that did not indicate ability—Blacks' performance rose to match that of equally skilled Whites. Additional experiments that minimized the stereotype threat endemic to stan-dardized tests also resulted in equal performance. One study found that when students merely recorded their race (presumably making the stereotype salient) and were not told the test was diagnostic of their ability, Blacks still performed worse than Whites. (APA, 2006, para. 3)

These results make clear the need to combat this potential threat in at least two ways: (1) by examining how the classroom culture can per-petuate such stereotypes and (2) by helping students make choices that further their potential learning capacity and undermine such stereotypes. You can help them do this by examining behavior or activity patterns you notice, providing feedback about those patterns, and encourag-ing them to talk about how they feel about their learning. Too often, students have received the message that they can't do something well. Over time, they internalize this feedback so that it becomes part of their self-concept. We can give students a means for exploring the roots of such beliefs by holding private conversations with them or reaching out to families to let them know what we are noticing. We must also ensure that our learning spaces work hard to honor the dignity of all students so that they are open to hearing our feedback.

Responsible Decision Making at the School Level

The importance of responsible decision making extends beyond the need to teach students the relevant skills. Schools themselves must model responsible decision making in the policy and program choices they make, including in such areas as ranking and tracking, curriculum, and ensuring students' social and emotional well-being.

Ranking and Tracking

A school's decision to maintain structures that rank and compare students, such as honor rolls or class rank at graduation, creates a social-emotional dilemma for students at every place on the lists. Structures that rank and compare students perpetuate the division between "haves" and "have-nots," rewarding the former and impairing the latter. They highlight the disparities and inequities between students who have families that can afford to hire tutors, pay extra for supplemental materials, or otherwise support them in everything they do, and students who do not have such advantages. These structures and their consequences need to be closely examined and reevaluated to answer the question of how we create a level playing field so every child has the opportunity to be successful. (See Chapter 5 for a discussion of the emotional toll of ranking.)

The decision to track students—even when we claim we don't do that anymore—also perpetuates a hierarchy among students and limits their ability to have agency over their learning. Leveled classes that require recommendations—such as "honors" and advanced placement (AP) classes—erect gates that determine who is allowed in. And because of the way the system is structured, a disproportionately low number of children of color or high-needs students are admitted. If we ever want to change this structure, we must consider allowing all students into higher-level classes and providing them with the necessary supports to help them be successful.

Curriculum Choices

As educators, we have an obligation to model responsible choices when we design our curricula. Too often, we maintain the status quo with the texts we choose or the versions of history we share. Too often, there are voices in history that are muted, for a variety of reasons. To be ethically responsible and equitable, we must attempt to represent all perspectives in a fair and balanced way; students need to know full stories, not just convenient ones. If we omit important elements, we need to be able to explain why. Furthermore, if we are truly committed to ensuring diverse perspectives, we need to welcome and include students in these conversations.

The function of school systems is to educate school-age children in the basics of reading and writing and in the content of various subject areas, and to turn out informed citizens to help democracy prevail. The curriculum is the piece of the system that determines what and how students will learn. School systems determine what content and skills need to be taught after considering their state requirements and looking toward future needs related to success in the world outside school. A systemic, or standards-based, curriculum seeks to provide clear objectives aligned with standards and assessment criteria.

In her book *Will Standards Save Public Education?* Deborah Meier (2002) locates curriculum with a larger construct of standards-based reform systems:

> Standards-based reform systems . . . are generally organized around a set of four interconnected mechanisms: first, an official document (sometimes called a framework) designed by experts in various fields that describes what the kids should know and be able to do at given grade levels in different subjects; second, classroom curricula— commercial textbooks and scripted programs—that are expected to convey that agreed-upon knowledge; third, a set of assessment tools (tests) to measure whether children have achieved the goals specified in the framework; and fourth, a scheme of rewards and penalties directed at schools and school systems, but ultimately at individual kids, who fail to meet the standards as measured by the tests. (pp. 5–6)

When I was a curriculum director, I learned that leading the decision-making process about what should be taught, how it should be taught, and how it will be assessed so that students acquire the content, skills, and depth of learning they need is a challenging undertaking. Working with the teachers and the assistant superintendent of curriculum and instruction, and considering the data from previous years as well as new state standards, we created a standards-based approach to improving the learning of all students. Along with organizing units in a manner that made sense, we wanted students to be able to practice skills and develop competency against standards by completing performance assessments with rubrics and other success criteria shared before the learning. The approach was intended to ensure equity and give students multiple opportunities to achieve proficiency or mastery over time.

O'Day and Smith (2016) emphasize the importance of broad support for school improvement efforts:

> The odds of success for a school with a population that has lacked important opportunities are substantially increased if it operates in a supportive environment where its internal (school) and external (district, state, and federal) leadership are all pulling in the same direction. This is the central tenet of standards-based reform, a systemic improvement strategy first articulated in the late 1980s and subsequently spread through federal and state policy across the nation. (p. 313)

Leaders must ensure that curriculum not only is written with an eye toward transparency for the public, since tax dollars are being spent to write it, but also is supported and examined regularly to ensure that it is serving all students the way it was intended to. As we implement our new standards-based curriculum, we want to make sure that it continues to serve its original purposes and objectives related to depth of learning for all students. The teachers who wrote the curriculum will need support throughout the year. Through classroom visits, informal data meetings after benchmark assessments, and revision opportunities, we can determine if the intended curriculum is what is actually being presented and how effective it is in helping students succeed.

The largest challenge concerns classes that culminate with state tests. One example is global history. New York State has recently redesigned the Regents exam around a new social studies framework that decreases the amount of content covered and focuses more on critical-thinking skills. Students will be assessed on their answers to questions grounded in a more thematic approach rather than isolated facts and on an enduring-issue essay that requires them to review and interpret a variety of primary documents with known biases and select the ones that support their ideas. Knowing that these are the skills the state is assessing, we realigned our curriculum to make sure students learn these skills and apply them in various ways, enabling them to make better decisions about how they study and write about their learning, not only on the test but also in the way they approach this kind of content.

I appreciate that this shift aligns better with interdisciplinary learning, an approach that moves beyond the walls of just one content-area class. Standards-based systems take skills and content and allow the teacher and school district to apply the learning as needed. Unfortunately, when state tests become the assessing mechanism, the hope of promoting a purely mastery system is challenged. For a standards-based curriculum to really work, the folks who write the curriculum must have control over the assessment so that the curriculum is appropriately aligned. This way, students can be involved in the decision making in class about what is taught and how, and they don't have to worry about a test that is being written by outsiders who aren't familiar with their experiences. Too much rides on the test scores in New York State, and teaching to a test deeply undercuts our ability to educate students meaningfully and deeply. The classroom needs to be a place where interactive, differentiated instruction engages students in material that can potentially make their lives better. If we want students to be successful, we must ensure that teachers are supported to help them be successful. According to Massell, Kirst, and Hoppe (1997),

> Policymakers must confront several immediate issues and challenges if they are to improve [standards-based, systemic] reforms. One . . . is the need to provide additional, and more sustained, support to teachers and local administrators. Teachers need access to richer opportunities on an ongoing basis, and they need direction and support from the central office staff. (p. 9)

The challenge with many reforms that occur in education—and standards-based curriculum is no exception—is that there are many different issues trying to be tackled with a cure-all without addressing the complexity of the issue. The only way we can improve students' learning (and decision making about their learning) is to make sure that the efficacy of the teaching staff is continually growing as well, not because the tests are changing and we are infatuated with the scores being printed in the newspaper. We need to focus more heavily on the relationship between what students need to learn and what they are able to do and what we are actually teaching them as it aligns with the standards.

According to the *Harvard Educational Review*'s review of Carr and Harris's 2001 book *Succeeding with Standards,*

> Although aligning standards with curriculum and assessment is necessary, in itself it is insufficient to achieve the linkage advocated for by Carr and Harris. Linkage requires that educators explicitly delineate the relationship between what students need to know and be able to do (learning standards), how learning is expected to occur (curriculum), and how progress is measured (assessment). It also requires that they delineate the relationship between the standards and other parts of the educational system. (T. M. B., 2001, para. 3)

Standards-based curriculum on its own is not a bad thing. Once we determine who the experts are who should be writing the standards and determining what classroom instruction looks like, then we can create assessments that support the needs of students based on what they know and can do. We can also include students in making decisions around their needs and develop classroom learning experiences that support those needs. Then students can continue to advocate for their learning and contribute to the curriculum for themselves and future learners.

As curriculum leaders, it is our job to make sure that the intended curriculum is centered around essential questions, is aligned with standards, delineates a skill set, and predetermines the kinds of assessments involving student choice and voice in the process. Then we can review data and adjust accordingly. This system was created to try to build more equity into the learning experience and provide more flexibility for students.

Having unbiased standards and core competencies that were agreed upon helps teachers, students, leaders, and families know the expectations and work toward a greater well-rounded level of proficiency or mastery. And when students know and understand their own levels of mastery, they are able to make better decisions about the kinds of learning environments they want to be in.

One School's Decision Making to Improve Students' Well-Being

Some schools have taken extensive measures to ensure the health and well-being of their students, particularly those who are under stress because of pressure to perform and attain perfection. Staten Island Technical High School (SITHS) is an example of a school that has used responsible decision making—often with student input—to implement significant changes that address stress-related concerns.

The school is a STEM-focused institution that the website Niche.com recently ranked as one of the top schools in New York State and the entire United States. Although principal Mark Erlenwein is understandably proud of the school's reputation for excellence, he also has recognized the troubling social-emotional issues that many students experience—not only because of school-related matters but also because of broader societal changes. As he explains,

> At a time leading up to the apex of our school's history, I found myself at a crossroads which required a deep look at what contributed to our school's success. More importantly, I also found myself leading the faculty through a journey of inquiry and change to address and fix the concerning trends which were a byproduct of our school and high-achieving students. . . .
>
> Our students are operating within a world of absolute information overload. They're challenged by the complexities of real-life blended with virtual reality, augmented reality, likes, follows, hearts, emojis, shares, [and] commentary. . . . They call this the era of hyper change and disruption. Albeit a school for gifted and talented, high-achieving learners, we were not exempt from the impact of this hyper change and disruption. We realized that as a school community we had to be resourceful in gaining insight into the mindset of our students, taking academic and social emotional data to quantify the source of the challenges and make honest, real and impactful changes in our academic setting and practices. . . . The tools to tackle this challenge required an innovative solution that identified and help[ed] quantify the cause-and-effect relationships behind the pros and cons of the academic numbers

game, with a focus on the social-emotional dynamic. (Erlenwein, 2020, paras. 1, 3, 4)

The school instituted a number of new procedures and policies. Teachers and other staff took advantage of a function of the school's learning management system that allowed for faculty to share anecdotal information about student behavior, forward it to administrators and guidance counselors, and document follow-up conversations with students and parents. As Erlenwein notes,

> Creating a live, on-demand, shared and searchable web of information centered around student social-emotional behaviors dramatically minimized the amount of time communicating on the who, what, when, and why of the details and empowered us to create solutions almost instantaneously. More importantly, this innovative means of data sharing and communication allowed us to begin to put preventative measures in place as trends were identified. (Erlenwein, 2020, para. 5)

Among other things, the system produced data that "showed increasing rates of lateness, absenteeism, grade obsession, fatigue, missing homework, academic dishonesty, and stress-related health concerns," according to Erlenwein (2020, para. 6).

The school determined that the most common stressors students were struggling with were assessment, homework, and grades. It developed new policies and practices to address each of these. The new approaches included limiting the number of full-period tests to no more than two per day and reducing the number of grading periods per term; fewer grading periods meant each period was longer, enabling more time for meaningful evaluation of student progress before high-stakes assessments. Teachers were given the option to make homework assignments voluntary.

Among the most significant changes were those related to grades. The school transitioned from departmental and individual course grading policies to a universal grading policy that used letter grades instead of a numeric grading scale and incorporated mastery-based practices that emphasize the "process" of learning. Students were allowed to request extensions for submitting work and could resubmit work based on teacher, self, and peer-to-peer feedback cycles that had occurred throughout the term. Academic components such as formative and summative assessments, classwork, homework, essays and papers, and so on, accounted for 85 percent of students' final grades, and the remaining 15 percent reflected evidence of "habits of success" such as timeliness and proactivity, participation and collaboration, character, and oracy.

Regarding the early implementation of these various changes, Erlenwein offers this reflection:

> [K]nowing that true impact with a higher fidelity of action and change will take several years, overall, the feedback was very positive and insightful. Students overwhelmingly appreciated the uniformity in grading policy, which leveled the playing field as to "which work" was "most important" to do. . . . With such a variety of "worth" among the grading [in] previous grading policies, decisions were certainly being made based upon "how much" something counted. Letter grades helped dull the sharp edges that pointed numerical grades facilitated. Students found themselves in broader groupings of academic success, where it mattered less how "specifically well they were doing" in points among one another, versus the importance of what they were learning. Students proclaimed that receiving an A– or B+ "stung" a lot less than receiving a score in the high eighties or low nineties. Teachers too noticed the initial positive impact of our collective changes and shifts in practice, with instances of academic dishonesty and stress-related health issues decreasing by 60% and 90%, respectively, in the first year alone. Interestingly, with "oracy" being among the Habits of Success that were evaluated throughout the school year, students responded with more quality verbal engagement in the classroom setting. . . . Seemingly, . . . our assessment of their oracy practices . . . encouraged a bit of an awakening among some of our more reticent and reluctant to speak students. (Erlenwein, 2020, para. 13)

Erlenwein (2020) notes that SITHS took additional steps "to further support the positive impact our overall changes had on students concerning stress" (para. 14). The school gave students access as needed to a "comfort dog" in the general office and in guidance counselors' offices. It also developed a mindfulness and guided meditation program for all students, faculty, and staff. Commenting on the importance of this program as a supplement to the "academic wellness" practices the school has initiated, Erlenwein says, "We feel strongly as a school community that our students, faculty, and staff could all benefit from a practice (meditation) that promotes body and mind, mental health and wellness, beyond the halls and walls of our school" (para. 15).

Erlenwein acknowledges the need to further refine and improve the initial steps SITHS has taken in response to social-emotional concerns, but he is pleased with the progress the school has made so far:

> All together, in a school community and environment where we were succeeding by all academic statistical measures, I'm in awe and proud of our faculty and school community for coming together to make changes that benefit the quality of life of our students, their families, and the faculty themselves. (Erlenwein, 2020, para. 16)

Final Thoughts

Making good choices is a skill we continue to hone throughout life, and as we get older, the consequences of poor decisions become more significant. No one is suggesting that we can prevent students' bad choices, and there is something to be said for learning from mistakes. However, if we can help students to understand right and wrong and to be aware of how their choices affect not only themselves but others as well, then we are doing them and everyone else a big service. Students need to realize that their decisions go beyond the immediate consequence and can have dire results for their learning experiences. By providing opportunities for students to make responsible decisions, we create space for them to take ownership of their learning and contribute to the outcomes.

Working together, schools and families can help youngsters make better decisions and ease the pain of poor ones when they occur. Rather than shaming students about the mistakes they make, why not refocus the conversation around making better decisions in the future? Give students the chance to regret their bad choices and outcomes, and teach them to recover quickly, building resiliency and the potential for deeper learning.

↶ Reflection Questions

1. How do I ensure students have opportunities to make good choices about their learning in my classes?
2. How do I react to student decisions?
3. How much ownership do students actually have in decision making in my classroom? How can I involve them more?
4. If tracking exists in my school, what can I do to ensure that gateways aren't preventing any student who wants to learn from being in my classes?
5. How can I make responsible curriculum choices that ensure all the voices in my classroom are represented?
6. How are my school and I demonstrating responsible decision making in the choices we make related to students' social and emotional well-being?

5

Understanding and Improving Emotional Responses to Grades

Grading students is a controversial yet time-honored tradition used in most school systems to efficiently communicate the level of a student's learning. Although it may be the most efficient way to share information, it is far from the most effective or compassionate way to do so. Kids at every level are labeled, compared, controlled, and ultimately dishonored by the process. Few think to question it because "it's how we've always done it," and perhaps they don't realize that there are other options.

Done well, assessment is a nuanced process that allows educators to really see where kids are in their learning, and it helps students and families identify and develop strategies for improvement. It can help all students develop a growth mindset (as described in Chapter 2) that allows them to feel successful as they progress from the starting point to the finish line in their learning.

In this chapter, we explore the emotional toll and academic segregation that grading promotes. Understanding that most systems and schools require grades does not exempt us from closely examining ways to improve our approach. Perhaps it is time for us to think critically about why these structures endure.

The Emotional Toll of Grading

Grading is an emotionally taxing experience for teachers and students alike. I can't say I've ever met a teacher, particularly a secondary teacher, who loves to grade work. That doesn't mean that they don't like giving feedback or helping students understand what they know and can do. It means that sitting down with a stack of papers to grade can be daunting. Additionally, the expectation of being graded and labeled is emotionally exhausting for students. First, it's the doing of the work and then, if they tried as hard as they could, it's the vulnerability of submitting their work to an audience of one—a person who has the power to determine if all of that hard work was worthwhile. Whether or not students have put forth their best effort, the work seems to define them and their teachers in an almost dehumanizing way, as high school student Logan Miller shared in an interview:

> When I get work, my first response to it is "What is my teacher's expectation?" Most of the time, they don't really make the expectations clear. I feel frustrated, so I reach out to my friends, who are also confused about what is expected, and then I feel both angry and fearful because I'm not sure if I'm going to meet the expectations regardless of how hard I've worked. Back in elementary school, when math started getting harder, I was always a good math student, but by 6th grade, the amount of homework had increased and my parents were taught how to do it a different way than my teachers expected. I didn't have a choice about how to do the math. Although I could do it in my head, I was expected to write it all out, and if I didn't, I'd be publicly ridiculed in class. I often cried at home when I'd feel paralyzed by not understanding how to complete the work in a way that I was told to when it didn't feel right to my natural process.
>
> My parents tried to help, but that only made it worse. It got to the point where my mom actually e-mailed my teachers and told them I was no longer going to do the work at home since I was already at 3 or 4 for what we were learning. I also got exempted from taking state tests at that time because of the anxiety it was causing me to do them. In 6th grade, the anxiety got so great that I started having panic attacks at home that made it hard for me to get to school.
>
> I told my teachers what was going on and so did my parents, I suspect, but they told me that I still had to complete the work like everyone else.

Now, in high school, I've had both positive and negative experiences with grades in my classes. Although I can achieve high grades,
I understand that I have to comply with my teacher's expectations in
order to do so. That doesn't always mean that I'm learning something
worthwhile, but it means I know how to play the game. During my first
set of midterms in 9th grade, I was stressed out that I wasn't going to do
well because it wasn't clear what we would be tested on in my different
classes. Once they revealed our grades, I did well and so felt relieved.

Logan's experience is common for students who are "high achievers." They put a lot of pressure on themselves to do well but often lose
out on the experience of joy in the intrinsic value of learning. As Logan's
mom, I've witnessed his anxiety firsthand. I've been called away from
my own teaching jobs to come and get him as he has been stricken
with panic attacks. Over the years, we've tried to work with teachers to
help them understand Logan better but often haven't had the kind of
successes we'd like. The teachers acknowledge that Logan is smart and
therefore think that pushing him harder is the best way to get the most
out of him. This isn't the case.

One teacher who really understood Logan was Ms. Abend, his
Project Extra teacher. (Project Extra is the gifted and talented program
in our district—another sore spot for equity.) She got to know him well,
building a solid relationship with him and encouraging him to tackle
problem solving in a way that made sense to him. Project Extra was the
only reason Logan went to school in 6th grade, and there were other
students like him in every class.

If all of us took the time to understand the emotional roller coaster
that grading creates and de-emphasized the practice, we would get more
out of all students. If we actively worked to teach and assess students in
ways that make sense to them, enabling each child to be successful, we
would have fewer students in a panic about going to school.

When I was a student, getting As was extremely important to me.
My struggle with perfectionism stole the joy out of learning, and I didn't
realize how much interest I had in certain subjects until years later, when
I wasn't competing with classmates to be "the best." I didn't often share

with my parents or my teachers how much stress I put on myself to achieve, but by the time I got to college, I already had an ulcer as a result of the stress.

No child should suffer physical ailments because of the anxiety and stress that grading can create. The psychological damage we can inflict on students unintentionally is also extremely dangerous.

Competition/Collaboration/Cooperation

Competition. It's a powerful idea that motivates and propels many of us in various ways.

I'm fiercely competitive and always have been. Having played many sports when I was a student, often as the only girl on an all-boys team, I clearly understood the level of skill I needed to attain if I didn't want to be made fun of or ostracized by my teammates. I never wanted my gender to define me or make them feel like I was the weakest link because I was a girl. As a result, I had to work even harder than my peers if I wanted to maintain my status and be a starter on the team. The same was true when I made the girls' varsity soccer team in my freshman year of high school. I knew I wouldn't get playing time if I wasn't as good as the older girls on the team, so I worked tirelessly during practices and at home to ensure I would be versatile on the field and could be moved around as necessary.

My competitiveness didn't only come out on the field; it came out in the classroom too. When exams were returned or projects handed back, all of us would gather to see who won the "prize" of the highest score. Eagerly, I would flip to the back page and promptly turn around to my friend Seth to see what he got. I would exclaim, "Ha! I beat you by one point *again!*"

Looking back on this experience, I'm a little embarrassed. After all, learning and sports, although they may be enhanced by some friendly competition, are really about collaboration. We need to be members of a team if we are to really grow as learners and players—especially if we want the play or the learning to be sustainable.

As teachers—the adult learners in a building—we may still experience uncomfortable levels of competition, whether it's about evaluations or program assignments or maybe even likability among our students. It's not popular to admit such inclinations toward competition, but they surely exist, the same way they do with our students.

That being said, collaboration is really the quality we must aspire to. Each of us offers a wealth of experience and knowledge, but not without a deficit. When we work with each other, our natural strengths are open to challenge and subject to improvement, and our deficits can be lessened. We are truly better together.

So how can you foster collaboration in your classroom and school? You must develop environments that prize people working together over ones that promote a winner. I'm not suggesting, however, that everyone should get a trophy. Instead, here's what you can do:

- **Get rid of grades.** Grading learning is a fairly ineffective way to communicate. It doesn't serve anyone. Learning is personal, and individual students do it from different starting points and at different rates. Encourage kids to compete with themselves, not with each other, to progress. Make learning about learning and *not* about being better than classmates or colleagues. If your school policy requires grades, you can reduce the number of graded assignments in your class and incorporate student voice in your assessment. For a deeper exploration of this topic, check out my book *Hacking Assessment: 10 Ways to Go Gradeless in a Traditional Grades School* (Sackstein, 2015a).
- **Offer opportunities in class for students to work together as a group.** Create group projects that require collaboration, and, in more informal situations, promote collective problem solving by giving students a challenge and having them work together to figure out a variety of solutions.
- **Define cognitive roles that go beyond mere "timekeepers."** In group work, roles such as "timekeeper" and "recorder" are helpful but passive. Students need to take on active roles as well. Make

sure that everyone has an opportunity to do some cognitive lifting, so that certain voices are not marginalized and others allowed to be more dominant. Connie Hamilton (2019) discusses things teachers can do to make sure students aren't passing the "cognitive baton" in her book *Hacking Questions: 11 Answers That Create a Culture of Inquiry in Your Classroom*.

- **Build relationships.** Give students multiple opportunities to get to know each other so that they can build trusting relationships (as discussed at length in Chapter 1). Collaborations are more effective when students know and trust one another. Notice that I didn't say anything about liking each other. Sure, that helps, but it certainly isn't necessary to be able to work together. A healthy respect goes a long way. In fact, sometimes friendship can detract from learning, especially among adolescents.
- **Don't assume that kids know how to collaborate.** Explicitly teach them how. Model collaboration with other teachers. Show students the outcomes of collaborative efforts versus individual ones.
- **Be transparent.** Not all collaborative efforts will be a success, especially not at first. It takes work to be able to succeed in a collaborative model because it is so different from a competitive model. Let students know that it's OK to lean on one another for help and to switch roles and share responsibility—but all of that takes practice. Always build in time for practice.

How Assessment Affects Self-Esteem

Students' self-esteem is often correlated with their understanding of how others perceive them. But by comparing themselves to others, they often miss the unique qualities they bring to the table and undervalue what they know and can do. Too often, their ability to achieve more depends on how they see themselves, and perceived success or failure in schools is a critical factor in their self-esteem. Many research studies show significant correlations between high self-esteem (including self-confidence) and high levels of achievement on the one hand, and low self-esteem and low achievement on the other. Promoting a culture that views mistakes as part of the learning process and encourages a growth mindset can help to mitigate the impact of perceived failure on students' self-esteem.

In particular, high-stakes testing has a major impact on students' perceptions of themselves. In the following commentary, John Castronova, school principal and cofounder of the Institute for Balance and Well-Being, describes the potentially devastating effects of such testing and urges educators to consider alternatives.

The Dangerous Intersection Between Assessment and Self-Esteem

The intersection of academic assessment and student self-esteem is a collision course. The educational field has long believed erroneously that testing is an accurate depiction of one's acquired knowledge. And this universal belief has led to teachers feeling the need to pressure students to perform well because it is a reflection of their ability to teach. This flawed reasoning has led to an erosion of the relationship between teachers and students. When test scores are used to denote understanding of the subject matter, students who struggle to retain factual information are labeled at-risk, slow learners, or students with a disability. The students who excel at memorization are believed to be excelling at understanding the subject matter. While these statements may be true for some students, too often it results in a false positive, a faulty conclusion with permanent consequences for the learners. High-stakes testing has only served to magnify the holes in this "cause and effect" reasoning between assessments and student learning. The result has been a devastating blow to the self-esteem of countless students who are labeled each year as "ones" and "twos."

Professionally, as an educator for the last 40 years, I have too often seen the negative impact of flawed assessment models on the self-esteem of students. Currently serving as the principal for a state-approved, private high school for girls who struggle with emotional challenges,

I see firsthand how traditional metrics of school success only serve to erode the social and emotional well-being of students. If not for teachers who are creative, flexible, out-of-the-box thinkers, these students would find little success in their emotional growth or their academic achievement. These students, and all students, need to have the opportunity to demonstrate what they know in an assessment milieu that suits them. Without that opportunity, they will perceive themselves as failures as reflected by their grades.

Personally, I have seen the devastating effects testing can have on a student who learns differently, as my daughter is a student with a learning disability. As a father, witnessing your child being crushed emotionally, day after day, week after week, year after year, by low test grades is to see your child losing their belief in themselves and their hope for the future. Traditionally, school systems are designed so that these students are made to feel inferior, or in elementary school vernacular, stupid. The unintended consequences of assessing this subset of learners are the students feeling like they do not belong, the teachers feeling ineffectual, and the school [being segregated] into general and special education populations.

We can do better to protect the self-esteem of our precious learners. We must break free of the illusion that testing scores equate to learning. If we step back for a moment and remember what the purpose of assessment is, perhaps we can reframe our efforts to ensure a valid result. Assessments should test what they are meant to test. If we want to know what students understand and can explain, we need to give them multiple opportunities to do so. We must first discover how our students learn and what modality they can best use to express their understanding.

As we have come to discover over the last decade, differentiated instruction is an effective methodology for all levels of learners. Differentiated assessment can be equally as effective as a means to assess what students know and understand. Teachers need to be given the tools to accurately measure the progress of all students, not just the students who are proficient at pencil-and-paper testing. If we use varied assessment methods, we reduce the risk of falsely labeling students as slow learners or, on the opposite end of the scale, superior learners.

Traditional multiple-choice standardized testing assesses a student's ability to succeed at taking traditional multiple-choice standardized assessments. Such tests may also tell you what a student knows and understands, but it comes at the expense of the self-esteem of far too many. Teachers need to be given the opportunity to use alternative means of assessment. The mental health of our students—all students—is at stake.

—*Dr. John Castronova, Principal, Harmony Heights School, East Norwich, New York,*
and Cofounder, Institute for Balance and Well-Being

Students' own thoughts about grades and self-esteem can provide valuable insights into this topic. Consider the following observations from Janani Nagasubramanya, an exiting 8th grader at Lawson Middle School in California:

I believe that grades and self-esteem are very much related. When a student looks at a test given, then and there the student's mental status will change for the whole day. If the test is easy, the student will be confident and excited to get a good grade and be proud of it. But this doesn't happen all the time to everybody. Especially if the student feels like the assessment given is not going to end well and the results are not going to be nice, it completely demotivates that person and lowers their self-esteem, . . . and they won't be able to do well in other classes where they are usually good. The student might have had challenges preparing for the test itself. So I was wondering, how would it be if teachers promote every student to the next grade level if they find some development and effort in them, even if their grades are not that good?

Personal Identity as Defined by Academic Achievement

Earlier in life, my self-definition as "an A student" was a huge part of my identity—and that perception continued even during my master's program and my early teaching career, so I can speak personally about the toll of academic labels. I wore my perceived successes as badges of honor, regardless of how that made others feel. Conversely, my brother, who is extremely intelligent, didn't "play" school well, and there were consequences for his lack of compliance. Our parents' expectations about what we accomplished in school varied widely. Over time, their expectations played into my perfectionism, and I felt additional stress to do well.

Conflating academic success with personal identity is perilous for students at any level of achievement. Many who are academically successful live with the burden of fear of failure and debilitating perfectionism, which can stifle authentic learning and creativity; some of them may not be aware of the effects, but the emotional highs and lows they feel during a marking period relate directly to their sense of their ability to continually achieve. On the other end of the scale are the students who struggle and are labeled as "stupid," "lazy," or "not strong." They come to believe that they can't do well in school, and some stop trying. The students in the middle are often lost unless they learn to advocate for themselves. Academic labels are dangerous and can hurt children in the long run, regardless of where they are on the achievement scale. Schools have an obligation to help all learners see themselves as capable and then create environments that allow them to thrive.

For a perspective on the damaging effects of linking self-identity with academic achievement, consider the following comments from Allison Hamilton, a recent high school graduate, about her learning experiences:

> Most days, I am a below-average person. Sometimes, I might get lucky and be an exceptional person, but most of the time, I'm far from it. You may ask, "What makes you mediocre, Allie?" My response would be, "I had to retake freshman biology, for the third time, as a senior." I wish I could look you in the eyes and tell you [that] everything about being a high schooler is what I perceived it to be. I wish I could tell you that I went into freshman year taking three advanced placement classes and graduated this year with honors. But instead of having that gold tassel around my neck, [indicating that] I finished with a 3.5 GPA or higher, I sit and realize that I am not good enough.

School has always been a challenge for me. I struggle with anxiety, so when I get a paper back and see the letter *D*, you'd think I wouldn't be shocked because I am pretty used to it, but every time, I break down, feeling myself sink into my chair.

Sometimes it's even harder for me when I do get a reasonable grade. When papers are handed back, I usually shove them in my backpack so no one can see, but on the rare occasion of me passing a test or quiz, I will display the paper in the middle of my desk, hoping everyone sees. However, deep down, I know I just got lucky. I know that there is absolutely no way I memorized the photosynthesis formula; the teacher must have made a mistake. But I also know, I'm not going to ask my teacher about it, because an *A* is an *A*, whether I earned it or not.

The past four years of high school have been a consistent cycle of cramming and failing. I don't know how the other kids in my grade do it. They get devastated if they get anything lower than an *A*, when . . . if I get a *B* my parents take me out for ice cream as a celebration.

Reading Allie's words made me feel extremely sad, because I know this young woman and she is exceptional. Too often, students allow their experiences in school to define who they are, to the detriment of their identity. If Allie didn't have to worry about being judged by her teachers and peers because of what she perceived as poor learning, she may have become more confident as a learner.

The lesson for us as educators is that we must work harder to make sure all students feel confident about their learning, even if they have not yet mastered content or skills. We can help them feel better about the learning experience both in and out of school by giving them opportunities to reflect on their learning and to develop a better sense of self based on individual progress. We can build celebrations into our learning environments that help students acknowledge their personal wins and the challenges they overcame to get to where they are now.

In an article titled "How Young Adolescents' Identity Beliefs Affect Their Learning," Dave Brown (2009) lists six identity categories that students may consider as they try to understand who they want to be and how that self-perception relates to their academic performance.

Those categories, and some of the related questions that Brown suggests students may ask themselves, are as follows:

- **Gender identity**—"What jobs might I hold based on my gender? How should males or females perform academically?"
- **Relational identity**—"How do I get along with family, friends, peers, and teachers? Which relationships mean the most to me, and how will those relationships influence my academic behaviors?"
- **Physical identity**—"Am I tall enough? Why is my hair dark instead of blond, curly instead of straight? . . . If I'm good at athletics, drama, or music, or if I am particularly beautiful, then I don't have to do well in my classes because in the end my grades won't matter."
- **Ethnic identity**—"What does it mean to be Chicano, Italian, black, Asian, Puerto Rican, Iraqi, Indian, or Native American? Are people of my ethnicity expected to do well academically?"
- **Oppositional identity**—"I don't want to act like the majority in a culture to which my family and I do not belong. . . . My teacher is white and my family doesn't think she cares about us. Therefore, I'll act in ways that reflect the opposite of what the majority culture expects."
- **Socioeconomic identity**—"Some of my peers wear clothing that is much more expensive than mine. . . . They live in huge houses. I'll never have what those rich kids' families have, no matter how hard I work. So why should I try?" (Brown, 2009, p. 1)

Brown also notes the following:

Teacher attitudes and actions also can affect student performance. Some educators explicitly or implicitly reveal their limited expectations for future academic success by their low-performing students through inadvertent comments. The way in which teachers respond to the language their students use in class (e.g., "Black" English or code switching among English language learners) can have a significant impact on whether students initiate the effort needed to perform successfully. And a lack of cultural responsiveness in teaching can compromise the academic identity of ethnically diverse students. (p. 2)

Brown's observations and the student voices represented in this book and in our classrooms remind us that we need to be aware of how our biases—even if unintentional—can harm student identity. To help students develop their personal identities, we must be relentless about exploring our own. We have an obligation as teachers to be honest about our own privilege and how that affects our work. So ask yourself, *How does my privilege affect my identity? How does my sense of self affect my students and my colleagues? What can I do to be a positive influence in students' lives? What would that look like in my classroom? In my school?*

Honor Rolls and Academic Ranking

Chapter 4 included a discussion of academic ranking within the context of responsible decision making by schools. Here we return to the topic to further explore the effects on students' emotional well-being.

Human beings should not be ranked in order of greatness, although we do so all the time, including via the long-held tradition of ranking students by honoring the top few for excellence in academic achievement. Unfortunately, when we select only a handful of students to recognize, we are simultaneously excluding everyone else. How does that help students develop into successful adults? Students who are not honored or recognized may feel overlooked and rejected and subsequently demotivated, even if they are otherwise thriving. Even those who end up at the top are hurt by this distinction because they may have prioritized academic competition over the development of meaningful relationships, intrinsic motivation, and interest in learning along the way. How does this approach prepare students for anything beyond possibly being disliked by their peers and providing their parents with bragging rights that will serve until their child gets into college and blends in with other "high achievers"? And how do these high achievers fare once they are among others who were declared "the best"? Simply put, if we turn learning into a competition that encourages students to fight it out until we name a few winners, we suck all the joy out of learning.

In an article titled "Academic Ranking May Motivate Some Students, Alienate Others," Jennifer Robison (2018) reports the following:

> Gallup research suggests that [rank ordering by GPA] might [improve performance]—and it might not. Academic motivation is complex and individual. Identifying each learner's unique, intrinsic strengths and building on them more effectively encourages academic success and, perhaps more importantly, engagement. (para. 5)

In his article "The Case for Abolishing Class Rank," Alfie Kohn (2016) argues that class rank, as well as grades, has a negative effect on many students. Among his arguments is the point that when we rank students according to grade point averages, the top students may be mere decimal points apart—a statistically insignificant margin that may unfairly make highly qualified students appear less desirable to college admissions offices. Kohn also notes that ranking isn't always based solely on academic prowess but may also reflect a student's "skill at playing the game of school (choosing courses with a keen eye to the effect on one's GPA, figuring out how to impress teachers, etc.) and a willingness to sacrifice sleep, health, friends, reading for pleasure, and anything else that might interfere with one's grades" (para. 11).

Schools need to reconsider their use of these practices and explain to well-meaning parents that maintaining such hierarchies only perpetuates cultures that segregate students and discourages a sense of true community. If we want all students to have a sense of belonging, we need to reduce the notion of academic competition and instead encourage students to aim for their best achievement as measured against standards of mastery.

Final Thoughts

Grading, comparing, and competing for rank can have negative effects on students' self-identity. Practices such as naming a class valedictorian or salutatorian promote a culture where only a few can be honored. In a more collaborative learning environment that promotes the notion that we are better together, teaching students how to function in teams is more productive than asking them to be "the best" all of the time.

The social pressures for attaining and maintaining excellence can put a serious amount of stress on children and affect their future in undesirable ways. The last thing we want is for students to be burned out on learning before they even make it to college. Peaking too soon can ruin, not support, careers and lives.

In the K–12 environment, we need to help students develop all the essential learning skills they will need to ensure future success, wherever their paths take them. Few students have their whole life journeys planned when they leave high school—and they shouldn't. Life offers many things to explore and experience, and cutting students off from possibilities can create more harm than good.

Reflection Questions

1. What have I done to ensure that my assessment practices are humane?
2. How do I feel about the importance of grades?
3. How has my experience in school affected the way I feel about myself?
4. How do I contribute to students' self-identity?

6

Reinforcing Student Dignity Through a Culture of Personalized Assessment

My teaching career began at Far Rockaway High School, located in a low-income neighborhood in New York City, with a student body made up almost entirely of minority students. Only four miles from where I had grown up in an affluent suburban town on Long Island, I was the only white person in the classroom. During those early career years, I learned a lot about myself. Foolishly, I believed I wasn't racist or biased in any way. My liberal parents had raised me to treat all people the same way, and I believed I did a good job of doing just that.

It wasn't until I really got to know my students that I realized I made assumptions that affected them negatively, as did my colleagues. I learned that I needed to have conversations. I needed to stay curious. I needed to challenge students, always treat them as capable learners, and elevate them—regardless of where they came from—to the heights of their own possibilities. The curriculum I was required to teach rarely addressed or spoke to the varied perspectives of the students I taught, and the traditional tests I was expected to give didn't provide the optimal opportunities for them to show what they knew.

I'm frequently reminded of my first students at Far Rockaway—intelligent young people who were often overlooked or treated differently than others simply because of the way they looked. When I moved to other schools in the city, I noticed similar situations, which never felt right to me. I always worked hard to try to take a different approach, making every effort to develop relationships with my students, understand them as people, and make better choices about how and what I taught so they would have every opportunity to be successful.

I have found that an important step in developing productive relationships with students is understanding the nature of our biases—particularly those we aren't even aware of. A good way to do this is through Harvard University's Implicit Bias Project, which consists of a variety of online tests that people can take to get a better understanding of what their implicit biases might be (https://implicit.harvard.edu/implicit/takeatest.html). I strongly recommend that leaders, teachers, students, and parents take a few tests to see what areas they need to be aware of and then work on improving those blind spots.

I took two of the tests when I was enrolled in a leadership program, to explore where I might have implicit biases that could affect my ability to lead with equity. The results showed that I have a slight automatic preference for European Americans over African Americans—a finding I would have never expected. I also learned that I have a moderate preference for light-skinned people over dark-skinned people, and that surprised me, too. Throughout my career, working in very diverse settings, I've tried to understand people, embracing their cultures and asking questions. I've been aware of my white privilege, which I've seen as a sore spot and sometimes even an embarrassment. Although I know I'm not responsible for where I was born or how I was raised, I have felt guilty when reminded that so many people are not as fortunate as I am.

As educators, we need to be acutely aware of our unconscious biases so that we can ensure that we don't discriminate in any way and that we make fair and equitable decisions related to both learning and assessment. Of course, "fair" isn't always "equal." We must give each child exactly what they need based on their experiences and personal learning preferences. We must adapt to our students rather than expect them to adapt to us.

Promoting a Growth Mindset in the Context of Assessment

In Chapter 2 we explored the concept of a growth mindset and its importance in helping students understand that it is OK for learning to take time. Students who develop a growth mindset know that if they don't acquire certain knowledge or skills right away, the inability to do so doesn't mean they are "slow" or "stupid"; it just means they haven't reached their learning target *yet*.

The implications for assessment are obvious. Many students view poor results on assessments as a form of adversity, something that may be too difficult to overcome. It is easy to quit when circumstances get tough, but we want our students to develop a growth mindset—a belief that they *can* overcome the challenge and succeed both in school and outside school.

Figure 6.1 illustrates how mindset affects a student's response to a disappointing grade on an assignment or assessment. It reminds us that

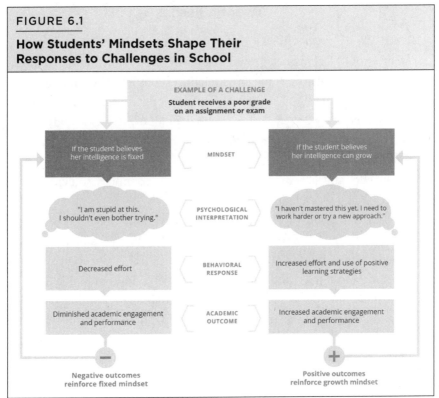

FIGURE 6.1

How Students' Mindsets Shape Their Responses to Challenges in School

EXAMPLE OF A CHALLENGE
Student receives a poor grade on an assignment or exam

| If the student believes her intelligence is fixed | **MINDSET** | If the student believes her intelligence can grow |

| "I am stupid at this. I shouldn't even bother trying." | **PSYCHOLOGICAL INTERPRETATION** | "I haven't mastered this yet. I need to work harder or try a new approach." |

| Decreased effort | **BEHAVIORAL RESPONSE** | Increased effort and use of positive learning strategies |

| Diminished academic engagement and performance | **ACADEMIC OUTCOME** | Increased academic engagement and performance |

— Negative outcomes reinforce fixed mindset

+ Positive outcomes reinforce growth mindset

Source: From https://mindsetscholarsnetwork.org/learning-mindsets/growth-mindset. Courtesy Mindset Scholars Network and Carissa Romero. Reprinted with permission.

we can effectively help all students develop a growth mindset by redirecting the self-talk we hear them using—to get them to see themselves as learners instead of being either smart or stupid. Students have so much potential to unlock, and we have many opportunities to help students connect with and explore that potential.

In the following vignette, a student tells how she was able to develop her growth mindset after facing the shock of failing a test. The account demonstrates the power of a growth mindset, as well as the effects that traditional grading practices can have on students who tie their self-worth to their grades.

Twenty Slashes

The thick, red slashes filled the page as my face flushed with embarrassment. I could feel my heart pounding in my chest as my mind imagined the entire class glaring at me, my straight-*A* status tarnished and broken. I stared at the lines in disbelief. No explanations were given, no feedback shared; only 20 red slashes to show for all my hours of studying and preparation. Unanswered questions swirled in my brain as I sat there completely perplexed. The large *F* glared back at me, taunting my intelligence and self-worth. I was no longer an exemplary student with a perfect GPA. I was a failure.

This was my first social studies test in 9th grade. I knew my notes well, yet the questions on the test asked about content I hadn't learned. I tried my best, but the questions confused me. It was as if someone had given me a test in a completely different subject. How could this happen? What did I do wrong? I was so confused and felt humiliated by the score on the page. I was frozen and paralyzed, unable to decide what to do. I'm shy. I don't ask questions, especially when I feel like I understand the information being taught. This test was different. It didn't match the lectures. It didn't match my notes. It had trivial facts about people and places I had never heard of before. As I sat at my desk wondering what to do next, the bell rang and class was done.

The next few weeks were a blur. My mom had a parent-teacher conference where the teacher admitted that the test came from a CD in the textbook, but she refused to change my grade or give me a different test. More tests were given, and I struggled with each one. It became evident that what the teacher taught in class didn't match what was on the test. My mom had another conference with the assistant principal and the teacher, but was told that other students were doing well, so the problem was with me. (They didn't know that other kids were cheating with the CD answers easily found online.)

Even though I was only 14, I quickly realized I was at a crossroads. I had never dealt with failure before. It hurt. It made me feel stupid. It was the one thing I worked so hard to avoid, yet here I was sinking in the quicksand in silence. It was then that I realized I had three choices: I could continue the year in frustration, take the easy road and cheat, or take ownership of my own learning and try to make the grade through perseverance.

I spent the rest of the year teaching myself. I took notes in class, then went home and cross-referenced them with my textbook. I visited websites and analyzed maps. I printed the state standards and made my own practice quizzes. I did everything I knew how to do to get an *A* in that class, then opened the envelope of my year-end grades to see the 92/*B* staring back at me. I didn't get the *A*. I would never be valedictorian. I might not get a college scholarship. There would be no record of all my hard work. No letters of recommendation would be written about my work ethic. No one would ever know how hard I had worked to master that class, except for me. Would any of that matter? Would anyone care? What did that *B* really represent?

Those 20 slashes in September cut me down like unwanted timber but became limbs of strength in the end. I realized that strength and knowledge are found in other areas, not just the numbers on a page. I became a self-advocate, asking for help when needed. I became a leader, sharing my knowledge with others. I learned how to balance my goals in life by joining clubs and playing a sport instead of focusing all my energy into schoolwork alone. I am still learning how not to be so hard on myself when failure appears. To fail is simply a *First Attempt In Learning*. I am greater than a grade on a paper. I am not defined by a red slash but empowered by the slashes not made. I can smile in defeat, knowing how to pick myself back up and get into the game. My first failure actually became my greatest success.

—*Katrina Letter, student at Christopher Newport University, future nonprofit leader of change*

Katrina's story illustrates the importance of nurturing a growth mindset in our students. As adults, we know that anything worth doing takes a fair amount of practice and time, and so we must remind students that learning requires tenacity. When we ask them to reflect on their learning, we should encourage them to go deeper than just their cognitive understanding of what they are doing and to also examine how they tackled challenging tasks and whether or not they persevered when it was tempting to quit. We can ask them to consider how they can more easily persist through challenging experiences in the future.

Careful use of praise in feedback is another strategy that can help students see themselves as working *toward* something instead of concluding that they are "not a math student" or "not a writer." In his book, *The Power of Praise*, Richard James Rogers (2019) suggests four basic rules for using praise:

1. Praise must be sincere.
2. Praise must be specific.
3. Praise must be recorded and remembered by the teacher.
4. Praise should be reinforced at significant points in the future.

Students need to know that we are paying attention, and when we use praise effectively, we show them we are listening, we are watching, and we care enough to notice and say something when all goes well. Of course, we must be careful not to overuse praise, which dilutes its power and makes it seem less sincere.

Building a Portfolio System That Documents Students' Growth

When it comes to fair, equitable assessment methods, standardized tests are problematic. Too often, standardized tests rely on context-specific content, language, and syntax that speak to a specific audience with a specific set of experiences—namely, white students. As a result, such tests can be considered racist, raising equity issues in terms of which students can be expected to score well on them.

In a 2003 article titled "When Learning No Longer Matters: Standardized Testing and the Creation of Inequality," Jo Boaler shows examples of how lower-performing schools that have the same or better achievement capacity as neighboring affluent schools in math aren't performing as well on tests such as the SAT-9. She argues that the test itself presents problems in the kinds of context being used to ask the questions as well as the way the questions are asked. In the article, which focuses on Railside High School, an urban low-income high school in California, she notes that when answering questions from an assessment "directly assessing the mathematics in the California standards . . . Railside students performed at a significantly higher level than students from other schools." Unlike questions on the SAT-9, the questions on this assessment "are not set in contexts that are confusing to linguistic minority and low-income students. Second, they reward all students who attain the correct answers, rather than only those who have answered the questions in the same form as the acceptable multiple-choice answer. Third, they do not use long and confusing sentences."

In addition to their shortcomings in terms of equity, standardized tests, as well as many end-of-unit and end-of-year tests, do not allow students to truly demonstrate what they know and can do, or their growth over time. For these reasons, we need to do better for our students, to consider other assessment methods. One good option is a portfolio assessment system.

Having students develop portfolios that collect their learning over time offers ample opportunity for them to reflect and track their progress, and it honors the work they have done. Portfolio systems, when successfully integrated into classrooms and school cultures, promote authentic student learning and assessment, providing visible evidence of progress that students and families can see. The system involves four steps: collection, selection, reflection, and connection.

Collection. The first step in building a culture that embraces portfolio assessment requires that schools and teachers clearly explain why students will be collecting their work. Students will be expected to maintain evidence of all their learning—completed assignments, reports, test results, artifacts, and other items—in a particular place, organized in a way that makes sense for them. Younger students can receive scaffolded instruction in how to gather and organize their portfolio components, with scaffolds gradually withdrawn as they become more comfortable and competent as learners.

When I began using portfolios, I had students place works in progress and finished pieces in hanging folders kept in crates at the back of the room. The collection process helped students visibly see their body of work, and it created a tangible record of learning beyond memories of tests taken. Eventually, we moved to a digital platform (schools can buy a platform or simply use Google Drive.). I showed the students how to organize their drive using folders and how to label their work. A bonus to keeping this digital is that the feedback remains in the document even after students resolve the comments and can be revisited for goal setting or reflection during the selection process; none of the work is ever truly lost. When writing hard-copy papers, students too often don't keep early drafts, throwing out the "practice" work as though it were somehow less valuable than the finished version. Digital portfolios ensure ease of collection and also have searchable features that make it easier for students to find what they are looking for.

Selection. A good time for the selection process is at the end of a grading period. As a class, you and your students can co-construct selection criteria—for example, choosing pieces that demonstrate best work or most progress—and determine how many pieces are appropriate. Then students can select the work that best meets the agreed-upon criteria.

Reflection. Asking students to reflect on why they made the choices they did, in writing or audio-video recording, helps them to articulate what they know and can do, presenting evidence from their own learning. Students need time to think about their selections, and the broader context of their learning in class, to develop thoughtful, coherent reflections. If reflection is a regular part of learning in your classroom, this step in the portfolio process will be familiar to students, requiring that they simply review the success criteria and articulate how the selected pieces meet the criteria.

Connection. The last part of the portfolio process involves making sure that students can transfer and connect their learning to different content areas, as well as to prior learning. You may need to provide some help to students at first, brainstorming with them to reveal how the learning connects to other content or skills they have developed.

Implementing a portfolio process allows schools to move away from traditional parent-teacher conferences that rely on gradebooks and conversations between adults, leaving out the most important voice in the conversation—the student's. Students need to be involved in the process so they can discuss their learning. Portfolio conferences and presentations are a great way to teach students to talk about their learning and prepare to defend what they have learned in a meaningful way.

Using portfolio assessment as an exit activity that replaces a final, timed exam is a step toward ensuring a more equitable, personalized approach to assessment. Students can review their learning over the entire school year and present their portfolio, demonstrating how their work aligns with standards and success criteria in all areas of learning. These exit portfolio presentations can be done in class for other students or before a panel of teachers. Another option is for students to make videos or screencasts to discuss their work. Figure 6.2 is an example of how I prepared my students for their final assessments.

FIGURE 6.2

Directions for Final Self-Assessments

It's the end of the year and time to really think about what you've learned. In preparation for your end-of-year self-assessment and final portfolio presentation, I'd like you to prepare a bunch of materials. Because there are several options for how you can present your evidence of learning, read the general information and then the part that specifically refers to your delivery method.

General directions

You will prepare your evidence of learning to show what you have mastered, or at least become proficient in, to supply your portfolio with evidence.

1. Review the specific standards for your class, as shown below.

   Standards for 11th Grade Newspaper
   http://www.iste.org/standards/for-students
   http://www.corestandards.org/ELA-Literacy/W/11-12/
   http://www.corestandards.org/ELA-Literacy/L/11-12/

   Standards for AP Literature and Composition
   http://www.corestandards.org/ELA-Literacy/RL/11-12/
   http://www.corestandards.org/ELA-Literacy/RI/11-12/
   http://www.corestandards.org/ELA-Literacy/W/11-12/
   http://www.corestandards.org/ELA-Literacy/SL/11-12/
   http://www.corestandards.org/ELA-Literacy/L/11-12/
   http://www.iste.org/standards/for-students

   Standards for 12th Grade Newspaper
   http://www.iste.org/standards/for-students
   http://www.corestandards.org/ELA-Literacy/W/11-12/
   http://www.corestandards.org/ELA-Literacy/L/11-12/

2. Review your work completed this year and the reflections.

3. Determine which work shows your mastery against the standards.

4. You should be able to show your learning in each of the core groups of learning, with specific reference to the assignments:

   a. Reading
   b. Writing
   c. Speaking
   d. Listening
   e. Language
   f. Technology

5. Make sure to indicate your areas of growth.

6. Did you meet your goals for the year?

7. What do you feel you could have done better? Why? How would you change this?

8. Make sure to grade yourself.

Explanation of grades

Grade	Level	Explanation
A	Mastery	Student makes inferences and/or applications that go beyond the simple and complex content that was explicitly taught. Student does the work consistently at this level without being told how to accomplish new tasks with associated skills.
B	Proficiency	Student demonstrates no major errors or omissions regarding any of the information or processes (simple or complex) that were explicitly taught.
C	Initial proficiency	Student demonstrates no major errors or omissions regarding the simpler information and processes *but* demonstrates major errors or omissions regarding the more complex information and processes.
P	Passing	With help, student demonstrates a partial knowledge of some of the simpler and some of the more complex information and processes.
ND/NI	Not demonstrated	Not demonstrated yet; student demonstrates no understanding or skills, even with help.

"+" = approaching the next level of the performance
Source: From *Classroom Assessment and Grading That Work* (p. 58), by Robert J. Marzano, 2006, Alexandria, VA: ASCD. © 2004 by Marzano & Associates. Adapted with permission.

Written assessment

If you are writing your self-assessment, make sure to comprehensively discuss the standards for each of the core areas and the assignments/ projects that address each of the sections. Make sure to write it like a reflection, with evidence from your work. Take screenshots to help show what you're talking about.

(continued)

FIGURE 6.2

Directions for Final Self-Assessments (*continued*)

Multimedia assessment

If you are using video, screencasting, or speaking (Voxer or voice message), I recommend you plan what you're going to say first.

In-person conference

If you are having a conference with me, you must come prepared with the above information and evidence. Think and prepare before you come for your scheduled appointment.

The conference schedule will be given out over the next week for each class. Those of you doing an alternative form of reflection, your work is due on _____.

If you have ideas about how to present the material, please don't hesitate to suggest them; no good idea will be turned down.

All prepared self-assessments are due on June 10th.

All conferences will begin on June 1st—the schedule to be determined.

After you have read these directions, please send me an e-mail to let me know how you will do your end-of-year assessment so I can plan accordingly. I should receive your e-mail **no later than May 19th.**

If you have questions, please e-mail me or ask me in class.

Personalized Assessment for ELLs

As mentioned earlier, a sense of belonging has a high correlation with student success—and, frankly, teacher success as well. Think about a time when you first arrived in a new job or school and didn't quite know where you fit. If you were fortunate, you quickly found a friend who helped you come into the fold, learn the culture and norms of the new place, and feel like less of an outsider. Students experience this need for a sense of belonging all the time, even when they know the environment they live in, so imagine how difficult it is for students who come to our schools from other countries who do not speak English as their first language.

It's hard to be an outsider. In the following vignette, I share an experience I had when visiting South Korea a few years ago. During this visit, I realized how isolating and even debilitating it can be not to be able to communicate what we know and can do. Language is a powerful tool that helps us really understand student learning and communicate new knowledge. Our kids who have come to us from other places have a wealth of knowledge that often gets lost in translation. As you read this account, consider how it feels to be an outsider and if you have any ELLs in your classes who seem to be struggling. What could you do to help them feel like they belong? How might you personalize assessment by helping them communicate their understanding?

Being the Only Person Who Doesn't Speak the Language: A Reflection

As I boarded the plane to South Korea to attend a conference, I had little idea what to expect. Just a month before, I had gone to Dubai for the first time, and aside from that, the farthest and most exotic place I had traveled was France, after studying French for more than eight years in middle school through college.

Although anxiety existed, my excitement for this new adventure overcame it, and when I got off the plane at my final destination of Daegu (more than a whole day later with the time change), I eagerly looked around, taking in each new sight, seeking out my new friend Jason, with whom I'd corresponded for months now.

Fortunately, he spotted me first. Not too hard to do actually, as I have purple hair and I don't look like the native people from that area.

"Starr Sackstein?" he asked, almost certain he was right.

"Yes, that's me. How did you know it was me?" I asked.

"I just had a hunch." He smiled warmly and offered to carry my bags, but I was fine as we walked to his car.

The weather in South Korea is a lot like it is in New York this time of year. Jason explained to me that the weather had just turned colder, and

I shared that the same thing happened in New York. It was sunny out, though, and the colors of autumn were all around us.

We eagerly chatted our way to breakfast in a place that he had never been to. I was nervous because my stomach doesn't always respond well to new foods, but I didn't want to seem ungrateful. The meal turned out to be fine, and interacting with my Korean guide and friend was interesting. I asked him dozens of questions about the cultural norms. Trying not to seem so surprised by what I was learning, I took it all in.

One on one, it was easy to be with Jason. His English is very good, and he went out of his way to be a great host. It was at this time that he told me he wouldn't be at the reception that night and that his colleague would pick me up and take me instead.

That first night after a long time spent traveling, I went to a lovely reception for the various important people attending the conference. I was the only American in the room and the only non-Korean speaker.

While I enjoyed dinner and the company of those around me, and several of the guests went out of their way to make me feel welcomed, I felt a little isolated. They all shared a culture, a language, and experiences as college professors that I couldn't relate to.

While sitting at that table and then at various other times throughout the weekend, I couldn't help but think about our English language learners who are new to our country, who know little or nothing about the language or the cultural norms. This was the first time in my life that I felt like an outsider in this way. In my youth, and sometimes in my adult life, I've felt different from others, but not unable to communicate. If anything, my ability to communicate who I am and what I stand for has always been a strong characteristic of mine, so I can honestly say that being without words was difficult.

Being in this position made me acutely aware of how isolating it is to not be able to understand a language. The people I was with were extremely accommodating, so it wasn't about that; it was about my own frustration with not being able to communicate in the language of everyone around me, who seemed to understand each other in a way I couldn't.

As I returned home from this new experience, I was left with some questions that need pondering in our situations at home:

- How do we engage students who are new to our country?
- Even if we are polite and welcoming, what do we do to help them feel less isolated?
- In what ways can we help them integrate without diminishing the importance of where they come from?
- How can we be more mindful of how we speak around them?
- Is our normal side banter more isolating if we do it around students who struggle to understand what we mean?
- What can we do to combat the loneliness of these students and improve their time in school?

As educators, we have an obligation to make school a safe place for all students. Children should know they can trust us and should never feel like it is OK to be isolated in any way.

The experience has profoundly affected my views for any marginalized group at school. One of our basic human needs is to feel like we fit somewhere, and if we don't feel safe in this way, the learning can never happen.

How can we engage our ELLs in our communities to help them adjust to a life so potentially different from their own?

Source: From "Being the Only Person Who Doesn't Speak the Native Language, a Reflection," by S. Sackstein, 2018, *Work in Progress* blog, *Education Week Teacher.* © 2018 by Starr Sackstein. Adapted with permission.

Faith Tripp is the ENL (English as a New Language) director and kindergarten center principal in West Hempstead Union Free Schools in New York. In the following vignette, she shares her tips on working with and assessing English language learners and multilingual learners.

Inviting English Language Learners into the School

New students arrive in our classrooms every day. They come from neighboring towns, from across the country, or from around the world. What every student has in common is the desire to belong, to feel that they are accepted as part of the learning community, and to be challenged to reach their full potential. Sometimes, it is a seamless transition that requires very little effort from the adults in the school. However, more often than not, our new students require that we go the extra mile to welcome them and advocate for their inclusion as well as ensure that assessments align with where they are right now and provide supports that help them experience success.

English language learners/multilingual learners (ELLs/MLLs) are often marginalized in our school communities. Their linguistic, cultural, and social-emotional needs must be addressed alongside their academics. As educators, we are responsible for advocating for our ELLs/MLLs to ensure that they are being viewed through an asset-based lens as opposed to a deficit model. We must ensure that our attitudes, language, and curriculum support a culture of inclusivity. We must maintain high expectations for all our students and provide multiple entry points and scaffolds to support their success, like providing assessments in students' native language and allowing for multimodal opportunities for students to show what they know. With just a little bit of planning, teachers can personalize instruction and assessment to meet the specific needs of their students. Co-teachers can and should work closely with their teachers and students to clarify and communicate each student's needs.

Educators should be cognizant of cultural practices that are typical to the student population they serve. It is critical to conduct research on your students' educational backgrounds and practices in their native countries. For example, many students come from communal learning environments that value group work and sharing. Allowing students to work together as they learn the new content and the new language promotes community in our classrooms and provides more opportunity for students to grow as learners. In the United States, individualistic beliefs are common, and educators are often suspicious of students who work together and help one another. They tend to view the communal approach as if the students were being dishonest or cheating, but the students are simply conducting themselves in a way that is both familiar and successful based on their academic experiences. As a result, educators should implement more communal activities; not only would that create a more inclusive atmosphere, but it is also a best practice supported by Lev Vygotsky.

Linguistic differences are another area to focus on when creating equitable, inclusive learning environments. ELLs/MLLs have the benefit of knowing additional languages! There are many cognates across languages that would allow an ELL/MLL to fully participate in learning. Simple supports like highlighting cognates take a few minutes during preparation but have a tremendous impact on student learning and feelings of acceptance. Every lesson should include opportunities for students to read, write, speak, and listen to support language acquisition. Visual supports are another simple but powerful way to help ELLs/MLLs enter the learning and find success. All these supports provide learning opportunities that we can use as formative assessment to offer more feedback and tailor learning plans based on what we learn.

Multicultural literature and representation is a must. Selecting read-alouds that depict students of various cultures, along with accurate representations of cultural practices, ensure that all students feel valued, recognized, and supported. When learning about math or science, it is necessary to highlight contributors from all backgrounds. Class novels should include authors and experiences from around the world.

Finally, be sure to include students' families in the learning. Invite them to share their culture in a way that is comfortable to them. Go beyond the annual multicultural night and include them daily. Find out how your students' families would benefit best from your support. Build the home-school connection and work together, across language and cultural differences, to create a truly inclusive learning environment.

—*Faith Tripp, ENL director and kindergarten center principal,*
West Hempstead Union Free Schools, New York

Final Thoughts

The better we know our students, the better we can personalize learning and assessment. And because we need to have good relationships with students to be able to assess them effectively, we need to create environments that honor everyone's dignity and provide a sense of belonging for all. Belonging is an essential need of human beings, and we need to foster cultures that prioritize it for the benefit of everyone involved. Before we can have successful learners, we must create cultures that develop a collective empathy for the needs of those supported within it. Regardless of the overall tone of the buildings and communities we work in, we have the power to create learning environments that seek to involve students and address their needs and desires. No matter who our students are, they deserve to be seen, heard, and considered when developing assessments so that we can ensure their success.

Reflection Questions

1. What strategies am I employing to ensure that all students have a chance to feel successful in their learning?
2. How do I help students employ positive self-talk around adversity when experiencing difficulties with learning and assessment?
3. Why is it important to include students in the assessment process?
4. How can I ensure that all students feel like they belong in my class?

Conclusion and Call to Action

School is so much more than teaching and learning. Each day, we have many opportunities to positively affect the lives of students. We can build relationships with them, support them in taking positive risks or exploring their interests, expose them to new and potentially life-changing activities and content, and promote collaborative environments where they learn to thrive as individuals and as members of a team.

Succeeding in this effort, however, means that we can no longer maintain traditional systems with one-size-fits-all curricula and assessment that consists solely of testing. The 21st century has proven that an approach to education modeled after the Industrial Revolution is a system that doesn't work for most kids. Some will succeed in spite of the way the structures are set up, but the vast majority will be marginalized in some way because of factors beyond their control—socioeconomic status, the zip codes of their parents or caregivers, the decisions schools make about placement, and the cultures within schools that inherently or unintentionally segregate students. If we are ever going to reimagine schools, we must do it with diverse voices and all kinds of learners in mind, starting with preservice teaching programs.

During the writing of this book, the world was experiencing a global pandemic and widespread protests against the systemic racism that has persisted in the United States since its inception. As a white educator who is always looking to learn more and to get better at finding solutions, I'm reminded of how much I have to learn.

My results on the tests for implicit bias, mentioned in Chapter 6, were an important step in the ongoing process. Coming to a realization of my biases has again raised my awareness that more action can be taken. I would like to seek out diversity training and continue to talk to people about their experiences. I've always been open to having frank dialogues with the people I work with and the students I have taught. If I don't understand something, I ask rather than guess. I try not to make assumptions about what people are thinking or feeling when they do something that I find troubling, and instead I want to dig deeper. What is the root cause? Are they having a bad day? Is their process different than mine? Am I having a bad day and therefore reacting more harshly or sensitively than I normally would?

In the world we live in, we can't get away from the implicit biases we bring to the classroom. We can effectively learn where our trouble spots are, but we need to continue to work, every day, on how we respond. If we want to reinforce student dignity when it comes to learning, we must create an atmosphere void of potentially derogative labels and meet each child where they are, always being honest about our own challenges and seeking deeper understanding. In this way, we can truly promote a personalized environment that can help us assess the whole child and give every person a sense of belonging.

Many of the voices presented in this book have helped me in areas that I still have to work on. In my years in the classroom, my students were always my greatest teachers. As I learned to quiet my own voice, I was better able to empathetically listen and then adjust my instruction for the needs of those who sat before me. Although I may not have called what I was doing "social and emotional learning" because I didn't have that vocabulary at the time, I knew that I needed to address the needs of the whole student and therefore to shift both instruction and assessment to meet those needs. It was no longer about the curriculum, per se, but about how to make the curriculum accessible to all kids, how to honor their voices, and how to help them be successful. Assessment had to be about learning and finding better ways to connect with students and to help them succeed in each situation.

It's time we make a real change in the way we assess our students, to recognize that they are a mixture of many feelings, strengths, challenges, and contexts to be explored and nurtured. We have a responsibility to do better for our kids.

What will you take away from this book that can positively influence the lives of the children and families you serve?

Appendix:
Sample Components
of a Course Syllabus

This appendix presents the following selected components from a syllabus that I distribute to students in the AP Literature and Composition course that I teach:

- Course Overview and General Information
    - Course Description
    - Objectives
    - Instruction Methods
    - Writing About Literature
    - Academic Expectations
    - Staying Organized
- Communications About Learning
- Assessments
- Course Texts
- Assignment Breakdown and Calendar

The complete syllabus also contains the following components *not* included in this appendix:

- A detailed outline of each semester's content, activities, assignments, and assessments
- The AP Nine-Point Trait Rubrics for prose analysis papers and poetry analysis papers
- A complete list of the Common Core standards addressed in the class

Course Overview and General Information

Advanced Placement Literature and Composition, World Journalism Preparatory School

Course Description

The yearlong, single-credit course in Advanced Placement Literature and Composition, while facilitating preparation for the national examination in May, strives to lead students toward greater understanding of the writer's craft through the close reading of complicated works from various genres, cultures, and time periods. Students will also rigorously prepare for college using this class as a conduit for time management and self-directed outside learning to supplement class-time activities. This class is for 12th grade students. It terminates in the AP exam that can yield college credit.

Objectives

Students of Advanced Placement Literature and Composition will

- Experience, analyze, and evaluate short fiction, novels, poetry, and plays from the 16th through 21st centuries.
- Build upon skills from previous English courses, particularly those involving written analyses.
- Recognize the significance of social and historical contexts, as well as an author's life experiences, when interpreting text.
- See genuine value in the manner in which particular writers employ figurative language, literary elements, imagery, irony, and symbolism.
- Consider how an author's rhetorical style conveys tone, purpose, and themes.
- Model fluency while drafting and revising a variety of written responses.
- Develop an engaging tone while writing, balanced in voice and grounded in parallelism and antithesis.
- Advance vocabulary skills to help cope with unfamiliar language.
- Develop the reading stamina and analytical prowess necessary to produce a well-written, properly cited and sourced 15-page literary analysis paper.

Instruction Methods

Discussion is the primary way in which students come to understand a particular text. Discussion occurs in both large-group and small-group settings. Discussions are usually student-led. Discussions are sometimes conducted online through Twitter and Blogger. Cooperative learning groups are also used extensively in this class. Projects/assignments will be done individually as well. Some assigned texts are to be read independently, in addition to other course texts.

Writing About Literature

- Students will write a variety of AP-style essays over the course of the year, most timed and completed in class. While all essays are expected to demonstrate general rhetorical excellence, each one has a particular thematic or analytical focus.
- Students will be writing to understand, writing to explain, and writing to evaluate. Quality of interpretation comes from depth of insightful understanding.
- Students are encouraged to revise essays as often as necessary.
- In addition to writing a variety of essays, students will keep a writing log over the course of the year to document their progress and to engage themselves in thinking about their writing.
- Students will also write reflective, more personal responses to literature throughout the year in study guides, etc.

Academic Expectations

- Complete all work on time. Extra credit will not be offered. You must have your assignments ready to submit when you walk through the door. If a printed copy of an essay is due, it must be printed prior to your arrival!
- The pace of AP Literature and Composition is fast, yet the scope is broad. Because this is a college-level class, students should strive to commit themselves to the study of college-level material and to discuss literature and other issues with maturity and decorum. Remember that, although effort is appreciated, it is not an indicator of grade. Your work will be graded on its own merit.

- Keeping up with the class while reading, researching, studying, and responding is key to success. This is a college-level course, and students who respect these parameters will earn reciprocal respect.
- Be present. Regular attendance is paramount! The intense climate and the quality of class discussions/projects are nearly impossible to duplicate in a make-up session. Therefore, student absences should be minimal.
- Be prepared. Show up to class and to conferences with current texts, drafts of writing assignments, and necessary supplies.
- Begin working when the bell rings.
- Keep bathroom visits to a minimum. Follow proper procedures for signing out.
- Embrace academic honesty. Please understand that whether it is a project, an assignment, an essay, a paper, or a presentation, all students are expected to submit their own work. Copying, or even using the work of peers to rephrase one's own answers, is considered plagiarism. Students are likewise responsible for properly citing sources in MLA format, even when they are paraphrased. This is very important. **Plagiarism is considered a cheating offense,** and it is against the rules and regulations. Students have nothing to gain through cheating, and everything—grades, college recommendations, and professorial trust—to lose. A signed plagiarism statement is required for all students.
- Read, reread, and read yet again. AP Literature and Composition is for dedicated individuals willing to spend ample time outside class poring over renowned texts and then writing about them. Revisiting particular works is not simply a suggestion; it is necessary in order for growth to occur.
- Go above and beyond. This expectation is demonstrated through student commitment to ongoing, thorough reading and investigative research, as well as a willingness to seek help when necessary. Before-school support is available, and each student will be meeting with Ms. Sackstein regularly for scheduled conferences.

Staying Organized

All AP Literature and Composition students need the following:

- A folder or section of a binder used solely for this course
- A spiral notebook or composition book for in-class note taking and out-of-class dialectical journaling
- A school I.D. and up-to-date school e-mail account, a Twitter handle, and a Blogger account
- Highlighters, pens, and pencils

Also consider having a personal copy of at least one of the major works studied in this class. Annotating your own text is a helpful study skill.

Communications About Learning

Writing assignments. The process of drafting and revising personal writing is an integral component to the AP Literature and Composition experience. It is important for students of AP Literature and Composition to make a personal commitment to growth beyond past written levels of achievement. Both instructor and peer feedback will be timely and elaborate. Specific areas of focus include the following: active versus passive voice, competent rhetorical style, subordination/coordination, varied sentence structure, effective organization, transitions, support, and commitment to subject, clarity, and voice. Please note that writing completed for this course will NEVER, EVER be a summary!

Class participation. Students must be involved in discussions, activities, projects, and review sessions. Such involvement will be regularly evaluated by both the instructor and the student.

Student-teacher conferences. These are a component of the class participation category. These conferences, held 10 times during the school year, afford each student the opportunity for a total of one hour of one-on-one, uninterrupted instructional coaching. Students are provided opportunities during the drafting process to get feedback based on specific lessons we've discussed in class.

Literature/poetry reaction papers. At the end of each week, in response to your reading, a 1- to 2-page typed and double-spaced reaction paper will be due on your lit blogs. Students will be expected to read and comment on one another's blogs.

Assessments

Assessment rubrics. All writing will be assessed using the AP rubrics, which are included in this syllabus. Most of the learning will be assessed against standards and using specific feedback personalized for the learner.

Timeliness. All written assignments must be completed on time.

Plagiarism. Plagiarism is the use of someone else's words, key phrases, or ideas without giving proper credit. This includes paraphrasing a source without giving due credit. Plagiarism is a serious breach of academic integrity, and any assignment containing plagiarism will not be accepted. Students will be issued a second assignment to be done in class.

Course Texts (subject to change)

Lit: Literature and Interpretive Techniques, by Wilfred L. Guerin and Michael L. Hall

Animal Farm by George Orwell

"A Modest Proposal" by Jonathan Swift

Gulliver's Travels by Jonathan Swift

Beloved by Toni Morrison

The Great Gatsby by F. Scott Fitzgerald

Invisible Man by Ralph Ellison

Pride and Prejudice by Jane Austen

The House on Mango Street by Sandra Cisneros

A Raisin in the Sun by Lorraine Hansberry

Hamlet by William Shakespeare

Rosencrantz and Guildenstern Are Dead by Tom Stoppard

Assorted self-selected novels/drama from the AP list for independent work

Assignment Breakdown and Calendar

- Please visit the website for supplemental materials and readings.
- Individual assignment sheets will be provided for all assignments.

Sep 9	First day of school—1st semester begins.
Sep 12	College résumés due
Sep 17	Meet the Teacher Night—please encourage your parents/guardians to attend.
Sep 19	Reaction paper #1 is to be posted on your blog.
Sep 19	First draft of college essay is due—conferences to follow individually.
Sep 26	Poetry reaction paper #1 due
Sep 30	Final college essay due
Oct 1	Poetry tutorial due—to be presented in class
Oct 3	Reaction paper #2 due
Oct 10	Poetry reaction paper #2 due
Oct 13	Columbus Day—no school
Oct 14	Read *Animal Farm* for class on Tuesday.
Oct 15	PSAT day—no class Senior group class photo
Oct 17	Poetry analysis paper due
Oct 17	Reaction paper #3 due
Oct 21-23	*Animal Farm* talk show chapter segments
Oct 24	*Animal Farm* in-class free response essay Poetry reaction paper #3 due
Oct 27	Begin "A Modest Proposal"—read for class.
Oct 31	Reaction paper #4 due
Nov 3	Read Part 1 of *Gulliver's Travels*—have it read for class discussion.
Nov 4	Election Day—no school
Nov 5	Portfolio Conferences—Night 5-8 p.m.
Nov 7	Portfolio Conferences—Day 12-2:20 p.m. Poetry reaction paper #4 due

Nov 10	Read Part 2 of *Gulliver's Travels*—have it read for class discussion.
Nov 11	Veterans Day—no school
Nov 12	Read Part 3 of *Gulliver's Travels*—have it read for class discussion.
Nov 14	Read Part 4 of *Gulliver's Travels*—have it read for class discussion. Reaction paper #5 due
Nov 17	CPAS—"A Modest Proposal" due
Nov 19	Prezi presentations for *Beloved* due
Nov 20	Read Part 1 of *Beloved*
Nov 21	Poetry reaction paper #5 due
Nov 24–26	Student-led discussions of *Beloved* begin International Feast
Nov 27–28	Thanksgiving break—no school
Dec 1	Read the rest of *Beloved*—have it read for class discussion.
Dec 4	*Beloved* short paper due
Dec 5	Reaction paper #6 due
Dec 8	Literature analysis paper due (3–5 pages)
Dec 12	Poetry reaction paper #6 due
Dec 19	Reaction paper #7 due
Dec 23	Talent show
Dec 24–Jan 2	Holiday break—no school Happy 2015! Read *The Great Gatsby* or *Invisible Man* and write a 3- to 5-page paper. The paper should be turned in in hard copy on the day you return (Jan 5).
Jan 5	Return to school *The Great Gatsby/Invisible Man* paper due
Jan 9	Poetry reaction paper #7 due
Jan 16	Reaction paper #8 due
Jan 19	Martin Luther King Jr. Day—no school

Jan 20	Begin study of *Pride and Prejudice* (Chs. 1–5). Please buy a copy of *The Annotated Pride and Prejudice* by Jane Austen, edited by David M. Shapard.
Jan 21	Read Chs. 6–14 of *Pride and Prejudice.*
Jan 22	Read Chs. 15–18 of *Pride and Prejudice.*
Jan 23	Read Chs. 19–23 of *Pride and Prejudice.* Poetry reaction paper #8 due
Jan 26–Feb 2	Regents Week—no classes *There is a chance that there will be a full practice exam one day this week—TBD.
Jan 30	Reaction paper #9 due
Feb 3	Read the rest of *Pride and Prejudice*—have it read for class discussion. 2nd semester begins.
Feb 6	Poetry reaction paper #9 due
Feb 13	*Pride and Prejudice* assignment due Reaction paper #10 due
Feb 16–20	Winter recess—no school Read *The House on Mango Street* or *A Raisin in the Sun* and write a 3-page paper discussing the author's craft in any three vignettes. The paper should be turned in in hard copy on the day you return (Feb 24).
Feb 24	*The House on Mango Street/A Raisin in the Sun* paper due
Feb 25	Read Act I of *Hamlet*—discuss Shakespeare, themes, anticipation guide.
Feb 27	Poetry reaction paper #10 due
Mar 3	Read Act II of *Hamlet.*
Mar 6	Read Act III of *Hamlet.* Reaction paper #11 due
Mar 9	Read Act IV of *Hamlet.*
Mar 11	Read Act V of *Hamlet.*
Mar 13	Poetry reaction paper #11 due *Hamlet* screencast due
Mar 16	Begin reading *Rosencrantz and Guildenstern Are Dead* (Act I). In-class conversation about adaptations and point of view

Mar 20	Read Act II of *R&GAD*
	Reaction paper #12 due
Mar 23	Read Act III of *R&GAD*
Mar 26	Evening portfolio conferences
Mar 27	Afternoon portfolio conferences—half-day of school
	Poetry reaction paper #12 due
Apr 3	Reaction paper #13 due
Apr 3–10	Spring break—no school
Apr 15	One-act play due
Apr 16–May 5	AP exam prep
May 6	AP exam
May 7	Research unit begins—go over assignment in class, reflect on the year so far, and self-assess and organize for research.
May 11	Critical theories unit begins. Readings will be provided online for you to print—refer to the website for specific nightly readings.
TBD	2–3 visits to the Queens College library to learn research skills and work on end-of-term paper
May 25	Memorial Day—no school
Jun 4	Brooklyn/Queens Day—no school
Jun 5	15-page paper due printed with all prior materials—final draft should be typed and double-spaced with justified text, be set in Times New Roman 12-point font, use one-inch margins, and include page numbers. Your name and title should appear at the top.
Jun 5–10	Jun 8—HS portfolio presentations TBD
	All work to be uploaded to e-portfolio with reflections; prepare presentations
Jun 16–26	Regents
	Jun 18—HS portfolio presentations 12:50–2:45 p.m.
Jun 25	Graduation
Jun 26	Last day of school

References and Resources

American Psychological Association (APA). (2006). Stereotype threat widens achievement gap. Retrieved from https://www.apa.org/research/action/stereotype

Arrabito, C. R. (2020). *Quiet kids count: Unleashing the true potential of introverts.* Highland Heights, OH: Times 10 Publications.

Bloomberg, P. J., & Pitchford, B. (2017). *Leading impact teams: Building a culture of efficacy.* Thousand Oaks, CA: Corwin.

Bloomberg, P., Pitchford, B., & Vandas, K. (2019). *Peer power: Unite, learn and prosper: Activate an assessment revolution.* San Diego, CA: Mimi and Todd Press.

Boaler, J. (2003). When learning no longer matters: Standardized testing and the creation of inequality. *Phi Delta Kappan, 84*(7), 502–506.

Brown, D. F. (2009, June). How young adolescents' identity beliefs affect their learning. *Middle Matters.* National Association of Middle School Principals. Retrieved from www.naesp.org/sites/default/files/resources/2/Middle_Matters/2009/MM2009v17n5a2.pdf

Chandler, D. (1995). Biases of the ear and eye: "Great divide" theories, phonocentrism, graphocentrism, and logocentrism. Retrieved from http://visual-memory.co.uk/daniel/Documents/litoral/litoral.html

Claxton, G. (2018). *The learning power approach: Teaching learners to teach themselves.* Thousand Oaks, CA: Corwin.

Cobb, F., & Krownapple, J. (2019). *Belonging through a culture of dignity: The keys to successful equity implementation.* San Diego, CA: Mimi and Todd Press.

Collaborative for Academic, Social, and Emotional Learning (CASEL). (2020). Core SEL competencies. Retrieved from https://casel.org/sel-framework

Costa, A. L., & Kallick, B. (2008). *Learning and leading with Habits of Mind: 16 essential characteristics for success.* Alexandria, VA: ASCD.

Costa, A. L., & Kallick, B. (2014). *Dispositions: Reframing teaching and learning.* Thousand Oaks, CA: Corwin.

Dell'Angelo, T. (2014, September 29). Creating classrooms for social justice. *Edutopia.* Retrieved from https://www.edutopia.org/blog/creating-classrooms-for-social-justice-tabitha-dellangelo

Delpit, L. (2013). *Multiplication is for white people: Raising expectations for other people's children.* New York: The New Press.

DiAngelo, R. (2018). *White fragility: Why it's so hard for white people to talk about racism.* Boston: Beacon Press.

Dweck, C. S. (2006). *Mindset: The new psychology of success.* New York: Random House.

Emdin, C. (2017). *For white folks who teach in the hood . . . and the rest of y'all too: Reality pedagogy and urban education.* Boston: Beacon Press.

English, F. W. (2010). *Deciding what to teach & test: Developing, aligning, and leading the curriculum*. Thousand Oaks, CA: Corwin.

Erlenwein, M. (2020, February 20). Academic and social emotional wellness for high achieving students [blog post]. Retrieved from https://markerlenwein.com/2020/02/20/academic-and-social-emotional-wellness-for-high-achieving-students/

Feldman, J. (2019). *Grading for equity: What it is, why it matters, and how it can transform schools and classrooms*. Thousand Oaks, CA: Corwin.

Freeman, Y. S., & Freeman, D. E. (2009). *Academic language for English language learners and struggling readers: How to help students succeed across content areas*. Portsmouth, NH: Heinemann.

Frey, N., Fisher, D., & Smith, D. (2019). *All learning is social and emotional: Helping students develop essential skills for the classroom and beyond*. Alexandria, VA: ASCD.

Gladwell, M. (2020). *Talking to strangers: What we should know about the people we don't know*. East Rutherford, NJ: Penguin Books.

Gorski, P. (2016). Rethinking the role of "culture" in educational equity: From cultural competence to equity literacy. *Multicultural Perspectives, 18*(4), 221–226.

Hamilton, C. (2019). *Hacking questions: 11 answers that create a culture of inquiry in your classroom*. Highland Heights, OH: Times 10 Publications.

Hammond, Z. L. (2015). *Culturally responsive teaching and the brain: Promoting authentic engagement and rigor among culturally and linguistically diverse students*. Thousand Oaks, CA: Corwin.

Hoerr, T. R. (2020). *Taking social-emotional learning schoolwide: The formative five success skills for students and staff*. Alexandria, VA: ASCD.

Honigsfeld, A. (2019). *Growing language & literacy: Strategies for English learners, grades K–8*. Portsmouth, NH: Heinemann.

Jagers, R. J., Rivas-Drake, D., & Borowski, T. (2018, November). Equity & social and emotional learning: A cultural analysis. *CASEL Frameworks Briefs, Special Issues Series*. Retrieved from http://measuringsel.casel.org/wp-content/uploads/2018/11/Frameworks-Equity.pdf

Kendi, I. X. (2019). *How to be an antiracist*. New York: One World.

Kohn, A. (2012, November 26). Homework: An unnecessary evil? . . . Surprising findings from new research [blog post]. Retrieved from www.alfiekohn.org/blogs/homework-unnecessary-evil-surprising-findings-new-research

Kohn, A. (2016). The case for abolishing class rank. *Psychology Today*. Retrieved from www.psychologytoday.com/us/blog/the-homework-myth/201612/the-case-abolishing-class-rank

Leland, M. (2015). Mindfulness and student success. *Journal of Adult Education, 44*(1), 19–24.

Love, B. L. (2019, February 12). "Grit is in our DNA": Why teaching grit is inherently anti-Black. *Education Week*.

Love, B. L. (2020). *We want to do more than survive: Abolitionist teaching and the pursuit of educational freedom*. Boston: Beacon Press.

Marzano, R. J. (2006). *Classroom assessment and grading that work*. Alexandria, VA: ASCD.

Massell, D., Kirst, M., & Hoppe, M. (1997, March 21). Persistence and change: Standards-based systemic reform in nine states. *CPRE Policy Briefs*. Consortium for Policy Research in Education. Retrieved from http://www.cpre.org/sites/default/files/policybrief/862_rb21.pdf

Mayfield, V. (2020). *Cultural competence now: 56 exercises to help educators understand and challenge bias, racism, and privilege*. Alexandria, VA: ASCD.

McDowell, M. (2017). *Rigorous PBL by design: Three shifts for developing confident and competent learners.* Thousand Oaks, CA: Corwin.

Meier, D. (2002). *Will standards save public education?* Boston: Beacon Press.

Mindful Staff. (2017, December 12). Disrupting systemic whiteness in the mindfulness movement. *Mindful.* Retrieved from www.mindful.org/disrupting-systemic-whiteness-mindfulness-movement/

Nelson, S. W., & Guerra, P. L. (2011, October). Cultural liaisons serve as bridge between community and school. *Cultural Proficiency.* Learning Forward. Retrieved from http://learningforward.org/wp-content/uploads/2011/10/nelson325.pdf

O'Day, J. A., & Smith, M. S. (2016). Quality and equality in American education: Systemic problems, systemic solutions. In I. Kirsch & H. Braun (Eds.), *The Dynamics of Opportunity in America* (pp. 297–358). New York: Springer.

Oluo, I. (2018). *So you want to talk about race.* New York: Seal Press.

Parsons, C. M. (2018, February 14). Sustained inquiry in PBL as a tool for social justice [blog post]. *PBLWorks,* Buck Institute for Education. Retrieved from www.pblworks.org/blog/sustained-inquiry-pbl-tool-social-justice

Ravesi-Weinstein, C. (2020). *Anxious: How to advocate for students with anxiety, because what if it turns out right?* Highland Heights, OH: Times 10 Publications.

Robison, J. (2018). Academic ranking may motivate some students, alienate others. *Gallup.com.* Retrieved from www.gallup.com/education/239168/academic-ranking-may-motivate-students-alienate-others.aspx

Rogers, R. J. (2019). *The power of praise: Empowering students through positive feedback.* Author.

Sackstein, S. (2015a). *Hacking assessment: 10 ways to go gradeless in a traditional grades school.* Cleveland, OH: Times 10 Publications.

Sackstein, S. (2015b). *Teaching students to self-assess: How do I help students reflect and grow as learners?* Alexandria, VA: ASCD.

Sackstein, S. (2017). *Peer feedback in the classroom: Empowering students to be the experts.* Alexandria, VA: ASCD.

Sackstein, S., & Hamilton, C. (2016). *Hacking homework: 10 strategies that inspire learning outside the classroom.* Cleveland, OH: Times 10 Publications.

Sheehan, K., & Ryan, J. (2017). *Growing a growth mindset: Unlocking character strengths through children's literature.* Lanham, MD: Rowman & Littlefield.

Starr, J. P. (2019, March 21). Can we keep SEL on course? *Phi Delta Kappan.* Retrieved from http://kappanonline.org/can-we-keep-sel-on-course-social-emotional-learning-starr/

T. M. B. (2001). [Review of the book *Succeeding with standards: Linking curriculum, assessment, and action planning,* by J. F. Carr & D. E. Harris]. *Harvard Educational Review, 72*(4). Retrieved from https://www.hepg.org/her-home/issues/harvard-educational-review-volume-72-issue-4/herbooknote/succeeding-with-standards_49

Tatum, B. D. (2017). *Why are all the black kids sitting together in the cafeteria?* (Rev. ed.). New York: Basic Books.

Tricarico, D. (2017). *The Zen teacher: Creating focus, simplicity, and tranquility in the classroom.* San Diego, CA: Dave Burgess Consulting.

Tricarico, D. (2018). *Sanctuaries: Self-care secrets for stressed-out teachers.* San Diego, CA: Dave Burgess Consulting.

Index

Page references followed by an italicized *f* indicate information contained in figures.

About the Author

Starr Sackstein started her teaching career at Far Rockaway High School in Queens, New York, in the early 2000s, eager to make a difference. Quickly learning to connect with students, she was able to recognize the most important part of teaching: building relationships. Fostering relationships with students and peers to encourage community growth and a deeper understanding of personal contribution through reflection, she has continued to elevate her students by putting them at the center of the learning.

During her first year as the Director of Humanities (business, English, library, reading, social studies, and world languages) in the West Hempstead Union Free School District in New York, she completed her advanced leadership certification at SUNY–New Paltz. Taking what she learned in classes and applying her classroom leadership to a team of teachers, Sackstein was able to start growing as a new school leader, building relationships and demonstrating the kind of leadership she wishes she had received earlier in her career. This experience inspired her to write *From Teacher to Leader: Finding Your Way as a First-Time Leader Without Losing Your Mind*.

Before her leadership role, Sackstein was a Teacher Center teacher and ELA teacher at Long Island City High School in New York. She also spent nine years as a high school English and journalism teacher at World Journalism Preparatory School in Flushing, New York, where her students ran the multimedia news outlet WJPSnews.com. In 2011, the Dow Jones News Fund honored Sackstein as a Special Recognition

Advisor, and in 2012, *Education Update* recognized her as an outstanding educator. Sackstein has discarded traditional grades, teaching students that learning isn't about numbers but about the development of skills and the ability to articulate growth.

In 2012, Sackstein tackled National Board Certification in an effort to reflect on her practice and grow as an educational English facilitator. After a year of close examination of her work with students, she achieved the honor. She is also a certified Master Journalism Educator through the Journalism Education Association (JEA). Sackstein served as the New York State director to JEA from 2010 to 2016, helping advisors in New York enhance journalism programs.

She is the author of *Teaching Mythology Exposed: Helping Teachers Create Visionary Classroom Perspective; Blogging for Educators; Teaching Students to Self-Assess: How Do I Help Students Grow as Learners?; Peer Feedback in the Classroom: Empowering Students to Be the Experts; The Power of Questioning: Opening Up the World of Student Inquiry; Hacking Assessment: 10 Ways to Go Gradeless in a Traditional Grades School; Hacking Homework: 10 Strategies That Inspire Learning Outside of the Classroom* (cowritten with Connie Hamilton); and *Hacking Learning Centers in Grades 6–12: Teaching Choice and Providing Small Group Learning Opportunities in Content Rich Classes* (cowritten with Karen Terwilliger). Sackstein has also contributed to compilation works, including *Education Write Now* and, most recently, *Ungrading: Why Rating Students Undermines Learning (and What to Do Instead)*.

From 2014 to 2019, she blogged on *Education Week Teacher* at "Work in Progress," where she discussed all aspects of being a teacher and education reform. She was a finalist for the Bammy Awards for Secondary High School Educator in 2014 and for blogging in 2015. At speaking engagements around the world, Sackstein speaks about blogging, journalism education, bringing your own device, and throwing out grades, a topic that was highlighted in a TEDx talk titled "A Recovering Perfectionist's Journey to Give Up Grades." Recently she has spoken in Canada, Dubai, and South Korea on a variety of topics from assessment reform to technology-enhanced language instruction. In 2016, she was named one of ASCD's Emerging Leaders.

Sackstein is currently a consultant with the Core Collaborative, working with teams on assessment reform and bringing student voice to the front of all classroom learning. Her affiliation with the Core Collaborative led to her position as publisher at Mimi and Todd Press, where she helps other authors share their voices around making an impact for students. Additionally, Sackstein is the host of AuthorED & InspirED, a video program of author interviews.

Balancing a busy career of writing and educating with being the mom of high schooler Logan is a challenging adventure. Seeing the world through his eyes reminds her why education needs to change for every child.

Rounding out her immediate family is her husband, Charlie, who is a mindfulness and meditation coach as well as a personal trainer. Together they travel the world, bringing harmony to each other's lives. Starr can be reached at mssackstein@gmail.com or via Twitter at @MsSackstein. She can also be found at http://MsSackstein.com.

Related ASCD Resources: SEL and Assessment

At the time of publication, the following resources were available (ASCD stock numbers appear in parentheses).

Print Products

All Learning Is Social and Emotional: Helping Students Develop Essential Skills for the Classroom and Beyond by Nancy Frey, Douglas Fisher, and Dominique Smith (#119033)

Cultural Competence Now: 56 Exercises to Help Educators Understand and Challenge Bias, Racism, and Privilege by Vernita Mayfield (#118043)

Giving Students a Say: Smarter Assessment Practices to Empower and Engage by Myron Dueck (#119013)

Mindfulness in the Classroom: Strategies for Promoting Concentration, Compassion, and Calm by Thomas Armstrong (#120018)

Peer Feedback in the Classroom: Empowering Students to Be the Experts by Starr Sackstein (#117020)

Relationship, Responsibility, and Regulation: Trauma-Invested Practices for Fostering Resilient Learners by Kristin Van Marter Souers with Pete Hall (#119027)

Rethinking Grading: Meaningful Assessment for Standards-Based Learning by Cathy Vatterott (#115001)

Social-Emotional Learning and the Brain: Strategies to Help Your Students Thrive by Marilee Sprenger (#121010)

Student Learning Communities: A Springboard for Academic and Social-Emotional Development by Douglas Fisher, Nancy Frey, and John Almarode (#121030)

Taking Social-Emotional Learning Schoolwide: The Formative Five Success Skills for Students and Staff by Thomas R. Hoerr (#120014)

Teaching Students to Self-Assess: How do I help students reflect and grow as learners? (ASCD Arias) by Starr Sackstein (#SF116025)

Teaching to Empower: Taking Action to Foster Student Agency, Self-Confidence, and Collaboration by Debbie Zacarian and Michael Silverstone (#120006)

For up-to-date information about ASCD resources, go to **www.ascd.org**. You can search the complete archives of *Educational Leadership* at **www.ascd.org/el**.

PD Online

Assessment and Student Success in a Differentiated Classroom (#PD14OC019S)

Fostering Resilient Learners (#PD19OC001S)

Grading Smarter, Not Harder (PD16OC005S)

ASCD myTeachSource®

Download resources from a professional learning platform with hundreds of research-based best practices and tools for your classroom at http://myteachsource.ascd.org/.

For more information, send an e-mail to member@ascd.org; call 1-800-933-2723 or 703-578-9600; send a fax to 703-575-5400; or write to Information Services, ASCD, 1703 N. Beauregard St., Alexandria, VA 22311-1714 USA.

WHOLE CHILD
TENETS

1 HEALTHY
Each student enters school healthy and learns about and practices a healthy lifestyle.

2 SAFE
Each student learns in an environment that is physically and emotionally safe for students and adults.

3 ENGAGED
Each student is actively engaged in learning and is connected to the school and broader community.

4 SUPPORTED
Each student has access to personalized learning and is supported by qualified, caring adults.

5 CHALLENGED
Each student is challenged academically and prepared for success in college or further study and for employment and participation in a global environment.

The ASCD Whole Child approach is an effort to transition from a focus on narrowly defined academic achievement to one that promotes the long-term development and success of all children. Through this approach, ASCD supports educators, families, community members, and policymakers as they move from a vision about educating the whole child to sustainable, collaborative actions.

*Assessing with Respect relates to the **safe, engaged,** and **supported** tenets.*

*For more about the ASCD Whole Child approach, visit **www.ascd.org/wholechild.***